A Guide to

Effective Communication

For

Conflict Resolution

A Guide to

Effective Communication

For

Conflict Resolution

How Mindful Communication
Supports Growth Through Conflict

Alan Sharland

CAOS Conflict Management Publishing
Caos-Conflict-Management.co.uk

To my brother Paul for reminding me of the kindness of my upbringing.

Table of Contents

Acknowledgements 9

How to Use This Guide 11

Principle 1: That we treat each other with respect 17

Principle 2: That we do not interrupt one another 39

Principle 3: That we have the right to pass 63

Principle 4: That we do not volunteer others 79

Principle 5: That we speak only for ourselves and speak in the 'I' using I-statements 97

Principle 6: That we speak, but not too often or for too long . 107

Principle 7: That we challenge the behaviour and not the person 121

Principle 8: That we respect confidentiality 141

Principle 9: That it is ok to make mistakes because they are opportunities for learning 153

About the Author 165

Other Publications by Alan Sharland 168

Connect with Alan Sharland 169

There is no such thing as a problem without a gift for you in its hands.

You seek problems because you need their gifts.

Richard Bach, *Illusions*

Acknowledgements

I would like to thank the people who have trusted me and afforded me the privilege of providing them with the mediation process or conflict coaching support since I started working in this field in 1994. Their courage and struggle to find a *better way forward* in their difficult circumstances and relationships have shown me the ways in which conflict can truly be an opportunity for constructive change and how the creation of open and honest communication can be the means through which it is achieved. It is through observation of their personal reflections and interactions that the Principles described in this Guide have been formulated and developed.

I would also like to thank my colleagues and friends in the field of Mediation and Conflict Coaching who have helped me to review and understand more deeply the issues involved in supporting others in resolving their conflict, and for their help in continuously refining the process we provide to help them do so.

Finally, I'd like to thank Tammy Gleeson for her patience and creativity in developing the cover for this book and Alan Jackson for his help with its editing.

How to Use This Guide

Welcome to *A Guide to Effective Communication for Conflict Resolution!*

This Guide is designed for use, initially, over a period of 9 days because it introduces 9 Principles of effective communication that also support conflict resolution and I would encourage you to focus on one per day to allow you time to develop awareness of the common ways in which they have an impact on interpersonal relationships. However, you may of course choose a different approach that fits more with your own learning style rather than feel constrained by the 9-day design, perhaps by allowing longer to explore each Principle.

If you browse through the Guide you may decide you do not wish to study the Principles in the order given and that is not a problem. They are not arranged in an order of priority as they all contribute to creating more effective communication. The interconnections that you will notice between them emerge more in a web-like fashion than sequentially.

Once the relevance of the Principles to everyday interactions are understood, you can apply them to your own communication practice and in so doing develop a greater consciousness, a 'mindfulness' about how you create communication in your life. It is likely that you will then find your ability to resolve your conflicts, have more meaningful and satisfying conversations, and your ability to support others in resolving *their* conflicts is also enhanced.

Footnote references to relevant content on the Communication and Conflict website (www.communicationandconflict.com), and some other websites that expand on the theme being discussed are given where appropriate. These are not essential reading for being able to use the Guide, but are given in case you wish to explore a theme further.

Some quotations from other authors or historical figures are from a time when the gender referred to was by convention male but I hope they can be read as referring to all.

There is a blank page at the end of each chapter so that you can make notes, or you may wish to use it to create a journal of your observations and reflections in relation to the Principle you are studying. Or you may just want to leave it blank - or take time out to 'doodle'!

Once you have worked through the Guide you can return to it as a reference in any difficult communication or conflict-related situation in order to understand how your own approach to the situation could be improved, or to help you understand the other person's perspective or communication more fully.

The practice of each Principle has its own particular impact on the effectiveness of communication and on the possibility of resolving any conflicts you are involved in. Some Principles may resonate with you more than others and some may be more difficult to practise in certain relationships - such as with your parents or with your work colleagues or your partner or children etc.

If that happens, *it is a gift just to be able to notice*, as that new awareness, the *mindfulness* that arises about your communication challenges in those relationships provides an opportunity for you to create more effective ways of responding using the Principles to help you. These situations flag up the real areas of being 'stuck' in our communication and relationships, so taking some time to work through them will enhance your ability to create effective communication and respond more creatively to conflict in many other situations as well.

The Principles of Effective Communication for Conflict Resolution presented in this Guide have been developed through observations and insights gained through providing mediation and conflict coaching, processes which are designed to promote effective communication and creative thinking in order to resolve conflict.

As a Mediator and Conflict Coach who has worked in a wide range of dispute, complaint and relationship-breakdown situations since 1994, I have not only observed common ways in which communication breaks down between people but also how that communication can be re-formed in a new, more effective, more personally satisfying way. My role is to assist people in creating their own more effective ways of communicating, and to help them create new ways of responding or behaving within their conflict so that the practical and emotional difficulties associated with it can be resolved.

This doesn't happen easily and sometimes it doesn't happen at all, but the obstacles to resolution and the communication mistakes become opportunities for those involved, and others, to learn from. This gives me a privileged opportunity to learn from those who I work with by seeing how they choose to recreate their relationships in a better form, and how they reflect on their communication breakdown and choose to improve it for the future.

As a Mediator and Conflict Coach I don't do that *for* people, I provide a 'space' in which they can take time for reflection and discussion and decision-making regarding actions they can take going forward to create a better situation and relationship for themselves. This gives me the opportunity to observe and marvel at the expression of the inherent capacity of the people I work with to heal their difficult relationships, communication breakdowns and unresolved conflicts.

Many of those observations, learnings and insights are presented within this Guide as the 9 Principles of Effective

Communication for Conflict Resolution you will now be introduced to.

It is important you use this Guide for application to *your own contribution to communication* and not as a basis for criticising others' approaches to communication if they don't seem to practise the Principles.

This is because there can be a risk of seeing the Principles as 'morally correct' ways of acting or as a 'set of values' which people 'should' live by, but I don't see them that way nor intend them to be read in that way. Their purpose is to support the creation of *effective* communication, communication that works in increasing connection, mutual understanding and the creative resolution of conflict. If we see the Principles as 'moral values' they would be more likely to be treated as 'rules' that *'thou must do'* and so, instead of supporting closer interaction and understanding they would become sticks to beat others with for not practising them, making them inherently inconsistent, self-contradictory and hypocritical in relation to their purpose.

Learning the Principles will help you to understand why some things that others say are uncomfortable for you but they also enable you to understand their perspective better rather than dismiss it. Dismissal of others' perspectives is a common response in a difficult relationship or unresolved conflict situation, and one which does not lead to its resolution for yourself or the other(s) involved. Starting to acknowledge and

15

'own' that we are dismissing their view and instead to become open to understanding it, even while not agreeing with it, is one of the first steps we can take towards creatively resolving our conflicts with others.

I hope you find the Guide and the Principles presented here to be interesting and useful and that they contribute to you having more effective, meaningful, and in some relationships, more intimate communication with others.

Alan Sharland

Clapton, London

November 2018

"Conflict is the beginning of consciousness"
Mary Esther Harding

So, let's begin…

Principle 1: That we treat each other with respect

This Principle invites us to reflect on, and acknowledge where appropriate, our own contribution to 'fuelling the fire' of an unresolved conflict even where we may see the other person as the aggressor, abuser, bully, demon or other protagonist with malicious intent. Recognising our part in this can lead to a significant reduction in the level of stress we experience in a dispute and in the time and energy we put into it.

Are you involved in a conflict that has not been resolved?

Perhaps it's with a work colleague, a family member, a neighbour, a partner, an ex-partner....

If so, consider the following:

- Do you treat the person you are having difficulties with disrespectfully? *For example, do you use sarcastic comments when speaking to them or about them? Do you have a 'name' for them that you use with others when talking about them - 'Little Hitler', 'God's Gift', 'Psycho Boss' or another term that is mocking towards them or derogatory in some way?*

- Do you make other negative comments about them when they are not present, or even in their presence?

- Do you find the conflict is leading to difficulties in other areas of your life? *For example, at work, with your partner, your children, at night before bed etc. because you are sometimes thinking about and talking about the person you are in dispute with and not about them?*

- Do you want the conflict to have less impact on your life?

It is rarely, if ever, true that people actually *like* being involved in an unresolved conflict, although people will sometimes say *'They love being in conflict'* about someone who doesn't agree with them over something.

This comment is one of the many ways in which someone involved in a dispute or other unresolved conflict can inhibit its resolution by not genuinely listening to and accepting that the other person has a valid perspective, just as they do - but it is a different one to theirs.

If a conflict is ongoing and unresolved it always means it is being responded to destructively in some way and therefore is a source of stress for those involved.

While we can tell ourselves it is justifiable to treat the person we are in dispute with in a disrespectful way, because of how we think they have treated us, it actually *makes the situation worse for us* if we do! We contribute to our own suffering and stress when we do this, but it is an extremely common behaviour, not just in day-to-day situations but amongst our politicians and world 'Leaders', and even in how *we* speak about *them.* You will also notice that it is the 'bread and butter' of a lot of media reporting online, on television and in the press.

Treating others disrespectfully serves none of us in a way that is helpful in reducing stress and resolving conflict such that we can *learn and grow* through the experience.

Why do I say that?....

Allies and Calls for Unity
Those who we perhaps think of as our allies, or who sympathise with us when we tell them about our dispute, may *expect* us to be disrespectful to the person we are in dispute with. They may even add their own critical comments.

You may also notice that when there are calls for 'unity' in difficult situations it is usually for unity *against* someone else, in which case it isn't really a call for unity at all but for division.

These common, but ineffective, responses to conflict, seek to involve others as allies *against* the other person(s) rather than as people who will help us to resolve it, those who *won't* take sides. When we meet up with our allies, they bring the issue up again and 'keep the pot boiling'. Even if we want a break from it at times our allies might think we are 'wimping out' or 'giving up' and so we have to be seen to be 'fighting on'. Sometimes it can feel as if our allies are fighting for us, perpetuating the disrespectful comments or actions 'on our behalf' – whether we have asked them to or not.

While it can be difficult to stop ourselves from treating the person we are in dispute with disrespectfully because we feel angry or frustrated or intimidated or some other negative emotion towards them, *it means it is __we__ who are perpetuating the conflict at least as much as they are*. And the consequences of our doing so spread to friends, colleagues, partners, children who either become directly involved as allies or they experience our stress and anger and fear and all the other associated emotions that come from a continually unresolved conflict.

It is commonly the case in disputes that people say the other person is the one *causing* them stress. But people often cause much more stress *for themselves* by doing such things as treating the other disrespectfully, whether in their presence or 'behind their backs'.

It takes a lot of time, commitment and energy...

- to try to belittle another person
- to denigrate them
- to seek allies against them
- to list for others the ways in which they have been cruel to us
- to outline the ways in which we have suffered 'because' of them
- to use up the quality time we have with our friends and partners or relatives, complaining about the other person and entrenching ourselves in our victimhood

I am not suggesting we should not talk about our difficulties.

What matters is *how we do so* and *what we use the opportunity to talk about them for!*

Look again at all of the above points:

- They are all setting out to demonise the other person or to pronounce our victimhood.
- They are not seeking ways of *resolving* the situation, or of *supporting ourselves in coping* with our difficulties with the other person and the situation we share.

- They 'recycle' our frustration, anger, despair, fear and stress about the situation rather than help us find a way out of these feelings.
- They are all manifestations of the *competitive approach*[1] to conflict that never works in actually resolving the situation.

Instead they all entrench us in the conflict, keeping *it* alive but draining the life from *us*!

Losing friends...

Seeking allies can also mean losing friends who do not wish to take our side because they, wisely, do not wish to be involved. They are not for, or against us[2], they just think it is up to us to sort out our dispute with another and don't feel they have to take our side in order to 'justify' our friendship with them.

Some people call that 'betrayal'. Some people say that means they 'don't care' and are not our friends after all. Some people even say that must mean they are 'against' us if they are not 'for' us. Many good friendships have been lost as a result of people holding that view and expectation.

---

[1] www.communicationandconflict.com/competition.html
[2] www.communicationandconflict.com/impartiality.html

But their not-taking-sides with us or against us is actually the most effective support we can have in the resolution of our conflict.

In many ways they are the truer friends as they are not judging us or the other person. They are simply being supportive if they are at least willing to listen[3] without taking sides. And they are more likely to listen to us if we don't put pressure on them to take our side.

We own[4] our dispute and our responses to it - and the consequences of those responses. Even those we say are 'bullies' are being spoken of negatively by us when we say that about them. We are labelling them and to challenge the person by labelling *them* and not *their behaviour* is an ineffective communication response to a conflict as you will see when you read about Principle 7.

I am not trying to say how you should act. I am just asking you: *Are you treating someone you are in conflict with - with respect? If not, what are the consequences for your situation and for others that know you and your relationships with them?*

---

[3] www.communicationandconflict.com/listening.html
[4] www.communicationandconflict.com/ownership.html

It is hard to resist the temptation to be disrespectful to people we have a difficulty with. Sometimes we will not be able to resist, but there are consequences that we can be mindful of and honest with ourselves about, and own the responsibility for when we are not treating them with respect.

You don't have to like the person you have a difficulty with, you don't even have to *feel* respect for them, but do you *treat* them with respect?

Only you can know the answer. And you will experience different consequences for yourself depending on whether you do, or do not treat them with respect.

It is tough to let go of the impulse to react disrespectfully towards those we are having difficulties with. We have put a lot of effort into making ourselves 'right' and them 'wrong'- but it hasn't helped.

The dispute still continues and leads to stress, it still pre-occupies us, distracting us from more pleasurable pastimes, from giving attention to our loved ones.

Just by recognising when we act disrespectfully, whether through our words, our actions, or just in our thoughts, we can start to respond more 'mindfully', with consideration for the consequences for ourselves and the situation rather than just react.

It hurts to spend our lives being disrespectful to others and so if there is a better way, is it not worth considering? For our sake, and for the sake of those we are close to!

We can gradually reduce our sarcastic comments. We can talk about something else with our friends. We can say 'hello' to the person we have a difficulty with, when we are in their presence.

It doesn't mean we have to pretend there's not a problem. We don't even have to 'try to like them'! It means we treat the other person with respect and separate them from the problem[5] so that we can then get on and deal with that!

I heard some of you reading that say: *'Huh but **they are** the problem!'*. If you did I ask you to consider if that is really so, or is it something or many things they have *done* which you have found to be the problem? Your wish to keep the problem located in an individual rather than focus on their actions is one of the ways you will remain stuck by devoting your energy to *demonising them* rather than use it to *support yourself* in the situation. The generosity of our friends and others' time spent

---

[5] www.communicationandconflict.com/challenge.html

listening to us can be spent discussing how to deal with the problem and not repeatedly demonising the other person.

The Principle *that we treat each other with respect* is about how *we conduct ourselves*, not about how we feel about others as if we should pretend that we 'feel nice things' about them.

This isn't a Principle that proposes denial or 'giving in' about something we feel strongly about. It asks us to consider how we are approaching our difficult situation so that the energy we put into it is used effectively and constructively towards something that works for us!

We can try to create different ways of responding that are more supportive of us and our situation and less exhausting than continuing with our disrespectful actions, words and thoughts which serve no constructive purpose for ourselves and those close to us who are also affected by our situation.

A couple of examples
As I write this section on *Principle 1 – That we treat each other with respect,* there has recently been a visit to the UK by Donald Trump, the President of the United States of America. A lot of publicity was given to abusive, mocking demonstrations by people who turned up at locations that he went to on his visit. There were social media postings of videos of people shouting abuse at him, there were placards with abusive phrases about

him on them, people were seen in videos laughing at the abusive comments shouted at him.

But I wonder if any of those who attended can see any constructive change as a direct result of the energy and time they put into the placard making, shouting, video making, posting on social media. I wonder how many are still spending frustrated hours doing so rather than putting their time and energy into creating something that will support them in the face of whatever they see his policies, behaviours and viewpoints as damaging as well as other challenges present in the world at the moment. I wonder how many are spending time in anger and frustration or feeling depressed because nothing seemed to change as a consequence of their actions rather than engaging with their children and loved ones, work colleagues and neighbours in ways that contribute to a better world as they see it, which can, of course, include being politically active, coming together as a community, creating new initiatives to support others and more.

For a short while it can feel 'good' to be disrespectful towards others we are in an unresolved conflict with because it gives an (ultimately futile) outlet to our frustration and anger, but in the long term **it hurts *US* when we don't treat others with respect.**

I often hear it suggested that 'Conflict resolution should be taught in schools as part of the National Curriculum' but I sometimes wonder who it is who will help children understand how to respond effectively to conflict when I don't see it practised as effectively as it could be in the adult world, and, as an ex-teacher myself, I don't remember there being a significantly greater understanding of conflict resolution amongst my ex-colleagues than there was in the wider adult population. Indeed, it was my own wish to understand it better while a teacher that started my journey into mediation.

But sometimes I do come across people who would fit the bill for that role:

Jo Berry is someone who, on hearing her story might be someone you would consider has more reason than anyone to treat others without respect, particularly members of the Irish Republican Army (IRA), and more specifically Pat Magee the man held responsible for planting a bomb that killed her father.

On 12th October 1984 an IRA bomb, planted in the Grand Hotel on the seafront in Brighton, a town on the south coast of England, killed 5 people and 34 people were injured. One of those killed was Sir Anthony Berry - a Member of Parliament and Jo Berry's father.

This is what Jo decided to do as a consequence of the murder of her father:

"I was devastated and shaken to my core by the pain and shock, I not only had lost my Dad whom I adored but I was thrown into a conflict and felt emotionally involved, I could not go back to the person I had been.

Just 2 days later I made a personal commitment to bring something positive out of it and to try and understand those who had killed him. I knew I had a choice whether to blame and stay a victim or take responsibility for my feelings and start a journey. I have known the pain that wants to seek revenge but have chosen to not act on this impulse, instead to work on transforming my feelings and end the cycle of violence and revenge in me.

In 2001, I first met Pat Magee the ex IRA activist/terrorist who was the only one who was held responsible for planting the bomb. He was released from prison as part of the Peace Process. I wanted to meet him to hear his story and see him as a human being. We had an intense first three-hour meeting, Pat started by giving his political position but half way through the meeting he opened up and became vulnerable, later saying my empathy disarmed him. Since then we have met over 80 times, sharing our story in many places and countries. Our first meetings became the subject of an award-winning BBC documentary "Facing the Enemy".

I believe we all have humanity in us and the way forward for a peaceful world is to give up projecting 'enemy' on to others. Instead we can learn to understand and to challenge behaviour through non-violence and peaceful means. If we can understand the roots of violence and conflict then we can address the underlying needs and find solutions which work for all. I believe we all have the capacity to be victims and victimisers, I know that if I had lived Pat's life I may have made the same choices."

Much more of Jo and Pat's story can be found at the website about their work:

www.buildingbridgesforpeace.org

I would thoroughly recommend attending one of their shared dialogues if you ever get a chance to witness one. Their meetings are not 'lectures' or speeches, but a simple, respectful dialogue about their personal histories and experiences particularly in relation to what preceded and now what follows that particular day in October 1984. Their meetings are not about 'how to forgive', as if a particular end point can be reached on such a journey, but they are an illustration of being able to treat each other with respect, even in the face of stark differences of background, values, expectations, experiences and events.

I don't know that I could do what Jo does now, but I can see that it is *possible* to do so and just hope I never have cause to experience the same challenge that she has faced.

When I provide mediation it is sometimes the case that one or both participants do not wish to meet the other person 'because of what they did' – and I fully respect that view. I would never agree with trying to coerce or persuade or push someone into meeting, including quoting Jo's example as a way of trying to 'emotionally blackmail' or 'shame' them into meeting. That in itself would not be treating them with respect. But knowing that Jo and Pat have been able to establish a journey of respectful dialogue that continues and develops, even to this day, shows me that no matter what has happened in a prior situation it is always possible to treat each other with respect.

Principle 1 Challenge:

If you are in dispute with someone, try to observe the following:

- How often do you spend time making negative comments to others about the person or people you are in dispute with? Or perhaps you even say the negative comments directly to them!

- How often do others bring up the topic of your dispute with you without you prompting them?

- How much of your day, how much of your energy goes into this?

Don't criticise yourself if you spend a lot of time and energy doing these things. Or perhaps you may even want to congratulate yourself for spending time doing so because you think the other person deserves to be treated disrespectfully.

Whatever your thoughts or feelings about doing so, *just notice your answers to the questions.*

This challenge is to become conscious of how you act towards the person, to become more *mindful* of your communication in relation to your unresolved conflict.

If you start to think *'Oh I shouldn't spend so much time thinking about them they're not worth it!'* - accept it! If you do, you do – just notice it. When you do, you do, when you don't, you don't - but just try to see how much time you are spending doing so.

There's no need within this challenge to try to stop yourself from doing this, as if fighting against your inclination to do so. It's about simply *observing how much you do it*, and looking at whether you can use your time and energy more positively to support yourself, first and foremost, in dealing with the present consequences of the situation.

A better relationship with the other person will be more likely to follow from you supporting yourself more effectively, so sometimes that's all you will need to do. It may not matter to you whether there is an ongoing relationship with the person but if you have started to treat them with respect and now focus the time and energy you previously used being disrespectful towards them on supporting yourself it will have more space to happen because it is not now being filled with sarcastic or belittling or other negative comments and actions.

The point is you are now using your time and energy more productively for yourself and those close to you and perhaps even for the 'wider world'.

If you are not in a dispute with someone:
Observe someone who *is* in dispute with another person, or group of people.

This can include observing a person, group, organisation or even a country and its representatives on the TV, in the papers, on the radio etc. Anyone you choose.

Consider the ways in which they speak about or act towards those they are in dispute with.

Do they demonise the others, portraying them as selfish, arrogant, a bully, rude, cruel, violent, 'less than human'?

Do they portray themselves as victims of the other's actions?

This is a manifestation of the *competitive approach to conflict* mentioned previously, in which we devote our time and energy to presenting ourselves as victims, rather than use that time and energy to seek resolution of our dispute or ways to support ourselves in the situation, whether we also see ourselves as victims or not.

This is not to ignore that there are clear victims of disputes such as war, and that terrible atrocities can occur to individuals in these situations. But the approaches of the representatives of the countries involved will almost always focus on demonising the other and emphasising their own victimhood and that of those they are claiming to represent.

And of course, the other side will do the same. This is done instead of focusing energy on seeking resolution and supporting those who have suffered.

For example, you will notice in many international conflicts there can be a condemnation of one side for using violence but there is not an acknowledgement of the condemning side's use of violence in return, or, if there is, it is 'justified' as being 'self-defence'. And of course, the other side says the same and so the 'battle' to be right and the other side wrong has no logical direction to go, other than in circles.

Outside of the situation you will see campaign groups set up to give voice to one of the sides they see as the 'victims', and soon, in turn, will be another group campaigning to voice the victimhood of the other side in opposition to the original group. In this way the unresolved conflict is extended, beyond the situation in which it is actually occurring, to others taking sides against each other, in other parts of the world, saying they are 'standing up for what is right'.

Demonising the other, not treating them with respect, is the *unconscious reaction* of most of us in an unresolved dispute. We are not 'wrong' or 'bad people' if we do this, it just doesn't help anyone involved, particularly ourselves.

Our greatest challenge and first step towards resolution is simply to become conscious of this response - to recognise that this is what we are doing. To develop a mindfulness about our communication practices.

When we recognise this, constructive change can happen through a focus on finding a resolution that supports ourselves first and foremost - not 'against' the other person but *for* ourselves. This can sometimes be all that's needed because we then feel less affected or upset, frightened or stressed about the situation. But if we can support ourselves first then we are more able, if we choose, to focus on resolution of the conflict with the other person.

This is far more likely to become possible when *we treat each other with respect,* even if that is not what we are *feeling* towards the other person(s) we have the conflict with.

Becoming mindful of our communication in this way helps us to *grow through conflict* and the development of mindfulness in relation to our communication practices will be a feature of all the Principles that follow.

That we treat each other with respect

Principle 1 Notes:

Principle 2: That we do not interrupt one another

Practising this Principle can have a significant positive impact on the willingness of others to communicate effectively, co-operatively, sometimes even joyfully with us because they appreciate the 'communication sanctuary' we provide for them through our commitment to creating a space in which they will be heard.

> **Seek first to understand, then to be understood** -
> Steven R.Covey

When we listen first and contribute later this has many benefits for the creation of effective communication:

- We hear *all* that the other person has said and so we are much clearer about what they mean than if we only hear the first 5 seconds and then start talking.

- We can relax and *just listen* rather than fill our mind with our reactive thoughts and assumptions about what is being said.

- The person we are listening to is more likely to listen to us in return as they are not having to compete with us to get their words out and are more likely to feel a sense that their message has been received.

In conversations about challenging situations such as a dispute or relationship breakdown where we may already have difficult emotions about the person we are interacting with, or about the topic we are discussing, these benefits are particularly significant because they support the resolution of any conflict within that interaction, simply because the communication created about it is more effective. The time and energy put into the interaction is used more efficiently in various different ways:

- People finish speaking much sooner than we imagine when they are allowed to speak without interruption.

- Less time is spent 'going over old ground' or 'going round in circles' because the topics for discussion are communicated more effectively in the first place.

- A feeling of trust that we will listen is more likely to develop towards us, and so the quality of our communication and the strength of our connection with the speaker increases making it more likely we will be able to co-operate rather than 'fight'.

When I speak of *connection* I mean a willingness to listen to someone else's view without having to agree with them. Often, in unresolved conflict situations there is a perception by one or all involved that to listen to another's view means 'giving in' or 'agreeing' with them or even that it is a sign of weakness to do so, and as a consequence little opportunity for creating effective communication is possible - a *disconnection* exists.

But interrupting can occur in other ways than just speaking over another person.

Sometimes we interrupt one another by 'thinking' over another person while they talk. Our thoughts can be elsewhere, either on something else entirely, or on our reaction to what the other person has said and our own thoughts and views and interpretations and assumptions.

This is the reason why just nodding and giving eye contact, often described as part of good or 'active' listening, means very little when we are in discussion with someone. Our thoughts can be elsewhere while we are nodding and looking at the person and so we may not really be listening at all!

This can be particularly true if we work with clients, perhaps in public services or the helping professions where we think we've 'come across this situation many times before' and so don't really need to listen to the (unique) detail of what someone is saying, but we've been trained that we should always nod and give eye contact!

Conversely, we may be looking at the ground, or even looking at a computer screen while someone is talking to us but concentrating fully on what they are saying.

Unfortunately, in many difficult conversations another significant interruption to listening is that the 'listener' can be more concerned with trying to interpret others' non-verbal 'behaviour' or practising all the 'non-verbal techniques' that can be read in books about 'body language' than with *what someone is actually saying*.

This kind of approach to communication has led to, or perhaps even comes from misconceptions such as the often-quoted 'Mehrabian Myth' - that 'Communication' is 55% non-verbal behaviour such as facial expression, 38% tone of voice and only 7% the words used[6].

Professor Albert Mehrabian, who did the research that is so often misquoted, said in an interview for BBC Radio 4 in 2009[7]:

"Whenever I hear that misquote or misrepresentation of my findings I cringe because it should be so obvious to anybody who would use any amount of common sense that that's not the correct statement."

---

[6] www.communicationandconflict.com/interpreting_body_language.html
[7] www.bbc.co.uk/radio/player/b00lyvz9 - after 23 mins into the programme

Attempts to 'interpret body language' distract us from actually listening to what someone is saying, even if the distraction it causes is going on in our head rather than an interruption through speaking over someone.

*Someone will know more about how well we have listened to them **from what we say to them after they have spoken** than from our non-verbal behaviour.*

If we can give a good summary[8] of what someone has said back to them after they have spoken, or, if we don't give a summary, other aspects of our response shows that we have listened to them *through using words they have used when speaking to us,* this will be far more significant than whether we have nodded or given eye contact, or whether we have sat or stood in the 'right posture' or had the 'correct' tone of voice or facial expression.

Rebecca Shafir describes true listening as 'being in a movie mindset' in her book – 'The Zen of Listening - Mindful Communication in the Age of Distraction':

> *The movie mindset is opposite to the act-like-you-are-listening approach, in which you mimic a listening posture, nod often, say "Mm-hmm," and maintain eye contact. How can you possibly make all these*

---

8 www.communicationandconflict.com/summarising.html

adjustments and still concentrate on the speaker? It is not that these actions are contrary to what you do when you really listen. But to focus on this list of body language to-dos risks appearing artificial to the speaker. Just like at the movies, when you forget yourself and get into the shoes of the speaker, your body naturally relaxes into listening posture. When you truly listen, you don't need to think about your posture or what you should be doing with your hands. Your gestures and expressions effortlessly reflect your interest. All you have to do is enjoy the adventure!

As with all aspects of effective communication practice, only *we* can know whether we are interrupting (with our thoughts) or listening well. And only we can control whether we are or not.

It's up to us whether we want to listen more effectively or not. No one else can do it for us or even 'make us' listen.

This is why the creation of effective communication through this Principle and the others has to be 'mindful'. If we simply apply a set of techniques like nodding or giving eye contact or having an 'open posture' but our thoughts are elsewhere on other things or on 'analysing and interpreting' the speaker's 'body language' we are not really listening at all.

If we are committed to creating a space in which the other person's contribution can be received and we are focused on what they are contributing, then we are effectively listening. We can go on to indicate to the person that we have listened, and increase the possibility for connection through summarising back to them what they have said using their words to do so, or by including and referring to their words within our own contribution that follows from our listening.

But what if they interrupt me?
If we think the other person is interrupting us, some people say that means we should interrupt them back! Just stop to consider for a second whether that will contribute to, or destroy the likelihood of more effective communication in that situation.

The Principles all relate to how *we conduct ourselves* when communicating, not how others do, or how we perceive them to be communicating. While we might feel the other person interrupts us, if we do it back it will be hard to say they are the ones 'who started it' even if we wanted to, and even if we could prove it the communication about the topic in question has already broken down.

If we stick to our own practice of this Principle – even to the extent of stopping speaking if we believe the other person interrupts us - we are optimising our contribution to the communication. This isn't because it places us on the 'moral high ground' (because we are then distracted by *that* and our self-congratulation will have stopped us listening) but because *it helps **us** the most* with what we want to achieve – the creation of effective communication! Our stopping reopens the space for us to listen to the other person so that we can continue to 'seek first to understand' and reaffirms to the other person that there is 'no battle to be heard in this interaction'.

It's important to note that in many unresolved conflict situations we may have a strong dislike for the other person we are communicating with, even to the point of hatred. The creation of connection with someone through giving them space to speak may not serve the purpose of us starting to 'like' them, indeed we may not be wanting it to, but it will serve the purpose of helping us to resolve the difficult situation we share with them. If a better personal relationship is wanted and is to follow it is much more likely to happen if we have seen that we can listen to each other and effectively resolve conflicts that arise between us.

Co-listening

I thought I would include in this section a description of a process that can be of enormous benefit for people in any kind of personal or working relationship which draws upon the practice of the Principle *that we don't interrupt one another* - a process known as Co-listening.

It is a very simple process - all the best ones are - and involves taking just 15-20 minutes out with a Co-listening partner to talk about a topic that is relevant to both of you. It could be:

- *'How my day went!'*, for example between partners who may find it difficult in their busy lives to find time to share with each other what they have been doing and how they are feeling.

- *'My thoughts about our project!'* for work colleagues involved in a shared project who may want to ensure they all have a shared goal and understanding of the project.

- *'How I feel about Mum and Dad's divorce!'* between siblings.

You may have other ideas for your own situations where Co-listening might be useful.

Co-listening helps to remove that feeling of *'Oh I wish I had time to tell (partner, colleague, parent, child etc) about..... but we don't ever seem to find the time to talk'...* or ... *'I wish I had time to sit down and listen to (partner, colleague, parent, child etc.), I feel like I'm losing touch with them and what's going on in their life.'*

The Co-listening process is as follows:
One person speaks without interruption for as long as they want about their day, for example, or their thoughts about a work project and their role and progress within it, or whatever topic they are wanting to co-listen about.

You may be concerned that I say *'One person speaks without interruption for as long as they want'* and worry that the speaking will go on for a very long time. If you are both really concerned you could set a time limit of perhaps 10 minutes for each speaker, but any shorter and there is a risk that one or both of you feels rushed and the point of Co-listening is to create an open space for speaking and being heard and not to set up a pressure to rush that.

It is unlikely that anyone will speak continuously for 10 minutes even if it feels like hours to the listener but you will find out when you try it whether you actually need a time limit. It is always preferable not to have one.

The other person *just listens*, with no commentary or questions while they are speaking, and at the end tries to give a summary of what the other person has said *in the words used by the speaker,* trying not to change or 'reframe' it. When reframing happens it can feel to the speaker as if what they said is not accepted or is being judged or even 'twisted' by the other person, or indeed it is *just not being listened to*!

It is also important not to give opinions or commentaries about what the person has said (*'It sounded like you were really angry'*, or, *'Well this is obviously a very difficult situation for you'* – it is important you **do not** do this). Just summarise back what the person has said, as accurately and as much as you are able using **their** words. This is helped by starting your summaries with *'You said....'*

For example:

> *You said you've had a really hard day at work.*

> *You said you've been feeling really tired and have been worried about whether you can get home in time to read to the kids before bedtime.*

> *You said that you miss me when you have been away on trips for work.*

It really is that simple!

The reason it is preferable to start with *'You said....'* is that we are acknowledging what has been said as the speaker's view without sounding like we agree with it or have a view or opinion about it. We will, of course agree or disagree or have opinions about what our Co-listening partner says but it is very important we don't include them in our summary. Co-listening does what it says on the tin – it provides *listening* – not commentaries, viewpoints, arguments, discussions, interpretations etc. Using *'You said...'* at the start of our summarising statements helps us to stay committed to that intention.

Partners then swap roles – the speaker becomes the listener and summariser and the previous listener now gets their opportunity to speak.

Note that no discussion of what the first speaker has said occurs between swapping round, there is just the summary and then straight into the swap.

Co-listening is not a test, so accept you may not be able to remember and summarise back some of what the other person has said, and they may not remember some of what you have said when they summarise your speaking. You may both make genuine mistakes in your summaries and you may both not recognise the issues and feelings the speaker sees as more important than others.

Co-listening is simply an attempt to give each other a chance to hear what you both have to say and hear it summarised back without judgements, opinions, advice, fixes, interruptions, comments and all the things that can get in the way of simply listening to what another person has to say and which prevent a feeling of being heard.

One of the reasons this is so powerful is that it is very rare in conversations to experience this simple reflection back of what we have said, with a reverence for *how* we have said it rather than have it changed or have assumptions made about what we 'mean' by the listener, or suggestions about what we may be feeling, or what we should be doing about something.

There is no interpretation within Co-listening, just a simple mirroring back of what we have said, as best as the listener is able to. What we also then find is that we come to a better understanding of *our own thoughts, feelings, perspectives, attitudes* about the topic we have spoken about through 'hearing ourselves' reflected back.

We also gain a better understanding of the other person through hearing them speak without feeling we need to 'interpret' and give a view or opinion or 'reframe' what they say or try to make what they say fit our own view of things. We can accept their expression of their viewpoint as entirely valid without needing to interpret it or change it or 'do something' about it, or try to 'show empathy' by guessing at what they might be feeling.

We could describe Co-listening as simply 'witnessing' the other person and being witnessed in return.

As has been stated earlier in relation to uninterrupted speaking and listening, Co-listening doesn't take very long *because* there have not been interruptions.

Sometimes the Co-listening ends there. There may not be time for anything further but it is a beneficial experience in itself because it has given that opportunity for connection and mutual witnessing that will perhaps not have had time to happen otherwise. The experience of taking out that 'special time' to witness the other person and honour what they have to say can have a very powerful, positive effect on the relationship between you both, whether professional or personal.

Sometimes, when there is more time, Co-listening is a great way of leading into an in-depth discussion, but it is important not to see that as a necessary next step. Co-listening is worth trying just by itself for the experience of simply honouring each other's thoughts and perspectives on the topic shared without the need to go further.

If a follow-on discussion is wanted, it can also be useful to have that some hours or even days later so that what has been heard from each other can be contemplated before going into discussion.

Co-listening is a powerful process which allows a full expression of thoughts and feelings about a shared relationship or topic, and the experience of hearing our partner, colleague, sibling, parent etc. summarise it back gives a real sense that they have connected with us at both a conceptual level and emotional level.

Whether between partners, work colleagues, school pupils or parents and children, Co-listening is an opportunity to create quality-time and highly effective communication.

With recent concerns about wellbeing and mental illness and the need for people to be able to talk about their feelings and concerns, this is a particularly relevant and useful process. It doesn't require a 'professional' to be our listening partner but of course it could still be provided by someone in a professional role. It can help to alleviate the sense that people can often have with professionals that they are not being listened to but 'assessed' with a view to being 'signposted' or 'referred on'.

Co-listening is an opportunity to just 'be' with someone and to have someone just 'be' with us, to witness us as we are, to hear our concerns and fears and aspirations and challenges but at all times to hear us respectfully and with acceptance rather than for 'assessment, diagnosis and prescription'. While that may sometimes be necessary, what people are often wanting is just to be listened to and the practices used within Co-listening, and which are very much represented by this Principle, are able to provide that.

You can use Co-listening however and whenever you want to.

Enjoy!

Listening within the mediation process

Within a Joint Mediation Meeting between two people who are experiencing a difficulty in their relationship or conflict over a particular issue (and usually both), we use 'uninterrupted time' at the start of the meeting to maximise participants' opportunity to 'mutually hear' each other.

One participant speaks about the issues of concern to them and how it has affected them and any ideas they have for resolving the situation, if any at that stage, and what they say is summarised back to them. This is then repeated with the other participant.

In a Joint Mediation Meeting it is the mediator who summarises back for participants what they have said so that they can just focus on speaking and listening.

Many disputes move closer to resolution simply through this part of the mediation process, without a discussion even having started, as participants start to realise that many of their assumptions about each other have been wrong. Participants may not have been able to realise this previously because communication has either not happened at all, or has been curtailed through interruption or shouting, abuse or ineffective, destructive argument and consequent misinterpretations and misunderstandings.

While this is not strictly Co-listening because it is the mediator doing the summary, and the discussion follows immediately rather than later, the benefits are the same and can have a transformative impact on the level of mutual understanding and connection between people when they are able to 'hear themselves' and hear each other without interruption, interpretation, opinion, commentary, suggestions, advice etc.

The Principle *that we do not interrupt one another* is often associated with 'being polite' or 'following etiquette' but its relevance transcends being simply a 'rule'. In the creation of effective communication its practice has a significant impact on our ability to connect with others and on supporting growth through conflict where one exists within the relationship.

A little tale to end...

When I first started working in the field of mediation I was employed as a Case Manager in a local community mediation service in London. One evening an elderly gentleman called up about a difficulty with noise he was experiencing from his neighbours above him in the tower block in which he lived. I listened for probably 5-10 minutes as he detailed his frustration and concerns and the events that had happened and his experience of contacting the local authority and other services to help him with the situation. I occasionally said *'Yes'* or *'Ok'* just to indicate I was still on the end of the line and at the end of his speaking I summarised back as much as I could of what he had said. That's all I did, but his response on my completing the summary was to say *'Thank you, you're the first person I've spoken to about this that knows what they are talking about!'.*

I explained to him that all I'd done was listened to him and said back to him what he'd said to me but he was quite clear that it had been the most helpful contact he'd made so far in his attempts to get support in his situation. I don't see that as being because of anything specific to me, but because of the discipline of approach that not interrupting someone and committing to just listening to them can provide, particularly when trying to help someone get their head around a difficulty they are experiencing and how *they* want to deal with it. We went on to discuss what he might want to do about his situation and he decided on some actions that would attempt communication with his neighbours. He didn't at that stage want to pursue mediation but the discussion helped him to formulate his own ideas for what he felt would help him.

Very often the bombardment of suggestions, advice, referring on, views and opinions that people receive when approaching services or even just friends who they want to listen to them do not actually help them and can, instead lead them to feel overwhelmed by their situation because of the additional complexity another's input 'throws into the mix'.

Many professionals are not trained to help people to help themselves which in many cases would be the most effective support they can have. Instead there can be an immediate assumption that the professional has to 'fix' the situation for people and so it becomes intrinsic to their practice to 'assess, diagnose and prescribe' even where that isn't what someone is looking for. A lot of professionals claim that is what people are always wanting but that assumption is something we will look at in Principle 4 where we see how our assumptions about what others think and feel inhibit the creation of effective communication and in turn, the resolution of a conflict or difficulty.

Sometimes people just want to be listened to and helped to reflect on their own ideas for supporting themselves, they don't want to be 'rescued' as that can lead to a sense of dependency and powerlessness. Where professionals only offer a 'fix' it is likely that a dependency arises in their clients as they are not being helped to create their own answers in their difficult situation. A similar consequence can arise if managers, parents, community leaders and others think they have to do the same when those they live or work with come to them with a difficulty. Listening and summarising – witnessing someone - is often the most powerful support we can offer them.

Principle 2 challenge:

Try spending a day observing yourself and others and consider the following questions:

- How often are you prevented from finishing what you want to say?

- What does it feel like to be interrupted?

- How do you react?

    o Do you 'talk back' over the other person?
    o Do you stop talking and feel 'put out' and undervalued, or offended?
    o Do you stop listening to the other person and wait for the smallest gap in their speaking so that you can slip back in with what you want to say?
    o Do you play the *'Can you let me finish!'* game where both you and the other person try to sound polite while continuing to interrupt one another?

All of these reactions prevent good listening and hence reduce the effectiveness of the communication we create with the other person.

Even our feeling 'put out' and undervalued or offended means it is likely we are not concentrating on what the other person is saying, and are focusing more on the uncomfortable feeling.

That's not a criticism, just an observation. We can't help what we feel. And if we believe people 'should' listen to us we are likely to feel that way.

However, what it leads to is a failure on our own part to listen to the other person. *Our reactions to being interrupted become interruptions of them and as a consequence we contribute to the breakdown in communication just as much as we believe they have.* Just notice if that is so. In some circumstances you may even find it funny. That's not a requirement however, just noticing is all that matters!

But also consider: How often do you interrupt someone while they are talking?

Whenever interruption occurs it inhibits the creation of effective communication, but we are more likely to be upset by, and try to control the interruptions of us by others than we are to focus on our own interruptions - and yet this is what we have most control over.

So, see how it goes to spend some time, a day perhaps, observing your discussions with others.

It can be interesting to note that even if we believe we are good listeners, our preoccupation with how 'bad' at listening someone else is will then distract *us* from listening - making us less effective than we could be.

As with all communication, it's our responsibility to maximise the effectiveness of our own contribution to its creation - whatever anyone else does! If we are focusing on what we think the other person is doing wrong, we are not focusing on making our own contribution to the communication as effective as possible.

And that's actually great news because it means it is in our hands to create effective communication and no-one else's. *We have the power* to maximise the effectiveness of our contribution to the communication we create with others.

When we focus on whether the other person has listened to us or not, we stop focusing on *whether we are listening to them!* As a consequence, our own listening is less effective and a vicious circle of non-listening occurs, leading to two parallel 'monologues' where very little, if any communication is created at all.

Try to always give space to others to speak even if you think they interrupted you! Instead of trying to talk over someone you believe has interrupted, stop to listen to what they are saying, however many times you think they have interrupted *you!*

I guarantee that if you do this they will eventually give you space to continue, particularly if you show you have listened to them by either summarising what they have said or, in your own response, you refer to what they said, using the words they used.

Some people see doing this as a sign of 'weakness' and that you should always 'stand your ground'. That may mean we feel we have been 'assertive' but it's very unlikely anyone will have listened to what we said, nor that we will have heard much of what the other person had to say.

I guess it's a question of what we think is more important.

Principle 2 Notes

Principle 3: That we have the right to pass

This Principle is about acceptance of another person's right to make their own choices, through recognition that we all have that right. In our interactions with others, the 'giving of space' to someone to be able to choose whether they participate in something or not can have an enormous impact on their willingness to 'open up' and communicate with us or whether they 'clam up' due to a feeling of being pressurised or coerced.

In my work as a Mediator and Conflict Coach I see how often a conflict will become and remain unresolved because there is not a recognition that *we have the right to pass*, to be able to say *'No'* to doing something that others may want us to do, or even expect of us.

Of course, there are consequences to all of our choices, whether we choose to do something, or, as with this Principle, we choose *not to* do something. Just as the choice is ours, the consequences that follow from that choice are also ours.

This Principle, in particular, highlights the fact that much of what makes up the day-to-day communication between people can be recognised as attempts to cause others to change, to be different to who they are - to try to control them.

Non-acceptance of the world *as-it-is* pervades much of what and how we communicate.

This Principle asks us to accept the world as it is. That's not an easy task and this Principle highlights how much our difficulty in doing so 'shows up' in our communication. It asks us to let go, to allow others to not have to do what we think they 'should' do. It arises through the recognition that *we* do not have to do what others think we 'should' do:

You must..... You've got to.... Why don't you.....? It's about time you.... I know what you should do..... Let me tell you ...... They should...

Such phrases are spread through much of our day-to-day communication which is why it can feel as if we are in a continuous state of 'attack/defend' in many of our conversations.

If you stop to monitor your own or others' communication you may be surprised to see how prevalent a controlling or 'unaccepting' mode of communication is present in everyday speech - one which is seeking to change another person or resisting change being imposed on us by others.

This is not a Principle of apathy, of doing nothing. It is a Principle of *active choice*.

The 'right to pass' is a recognition of our right to say *'No'* to anyone or to doing anything if saying *'No'* is what we truly wish to do.

This Principle is informed by an Underlying Philosophy of Mediation and Conflict Coaching, that of *Ownership*[9]. It allows, and moreover, it *expects* me to own my decisions (because who else can?) and when I consciously acknowledge this in myself it makes it much more likely I can accept the right of others to make their own decisions.

It is implicit within this Principle that I also take responsibility for, and 'own' my decision to pass on doing something and I accept the consequences of that decision, even if I can't foresee what they might be.

To lead the horse to water and accept it not drinking is to practise this Principle. It may not have been thirsty in the first place. Only the horse can know if it is thirsty. We may think we know it is thirsty, but the horse knows far better than us. In time, if we keep trying to force it to drink it could well 'up and run away'.

And so, we lose our connection - with the horse and with anyone we treat in a similar way by volunteering them to do something

---

[9] www.communicationandconflict.com/ownership.html

they may not want to do, or assuming that we know what is best for them. If we don't acknowledge that we all have the right to pass, to say *no* to someone if it feels right for us to do so, and that others have that right in relation to our own expectations and beliefs about them, then our communication and relationships will be very likely to suffer a breakdown.

The failure to apply this Principle is one of the main manifestations of the *Rescuer Syndrome*[10]. There will be other interpretations of the Rescuer Syndrome when it is used in other contexts but within the context of mediation and conflict coaching I describe it in this way:

Our belief that we know better than someone else how to resolve their conflict, or deal with some other situation in their lives, or are somehow better equipped to do so, leads us to intervene or try to 'rescue' them in a way which inhibits their ability to deal with their situation themselves. We may not acknowledge the right of others to pass on something because we believe we know what's best for them.

And we can cause ourselves a lot of stress, anxiety, anger, ill-health, frustration etc. simply because we don't acknowledge others' right to pass, to make their own decisions, or to not make a decision at all in the way we might be expecting of them.

---

[10] www.communicationandconflict.com/Rescuer.html

We can become addicted to 'making them change'
One of the biggest challenges in any family or other relationship where one member has an addiction or some other personal challenge is to learn to accept them rather than 'make them change'. Indeed, it can easily be seen to be the ones trying to 'make them change' that have as much of an addiction to that goal as the person considered to have the original addiction.

This is recognised by support organisations such as Al-Anon which supports anyone whose life has been affected by someone else's addiction to alcohol. There are similar support groups for people affected by another's addiction to drugs, gambling and other activities or substances.

The attempt to 'change' or 'cure' the person can lead to frustration for those trying to do so. Those with the addiction can experience guilt and resentment and a need to 'escape' and a complete breakdown in the relationship(s) involved can occur, leading to isolation for the person with the addiction and therefore less support for their recovery.

Offering support and simply being 'present' for someone with any difficulty is very different to trying to 'make them change'. One helps the individual concerned, the other is a taking-over of the person's life by someone who believes they can 'fix' them, as if they can 'live out' their life *for* them.

A true, *mindful* understanding of this Principle helps us to recognise the clear difference between these two approaches.

'Parent-Child' relationships

The challenge of acknowledging and practising the right to pass can be particularly noticeable in parents when their children are becoming adults. The belief that the parent 'knows best', and the reluctance to allow their offspring to make mistakes, to not follow their 'parental wisdom', can lead to intense struggles.

The young adult is not quite ready to fly the nest and simply walk away from the pressure to do what they are told they 'should' do, and so their only sanctuary is to close down and not let anything in.

And as the pressure mounts, the armour thickens and the connection is lost. Sometimes it is never regained because the child and the parents don't create a different and better way of communicating in later life.

But before we consider parents and teenagers a special case, the *Parent-Child* scenario can happen in all areas of life:

- The person who thinks their loved one *should* be different in some way - get a different job, be more active, lose weight, wear different clothes, work less etc.

- The boss who thinks the employee *should* try to climb the career ladder, go on a development course, be more assertive etc.

- The person who thinks their friend *should* find a partner, or stand up to their parents, make more of themselves, deal with their grief over a bereavement or relationship breakdown in a particular way etc.

Many of us have been there, perhaps all of us. There's nothing wrong with having the ideas.

But do we allow the other person the right to pass on our ideas for them?

Ultimately, we have no choice. But a lot of cajoling, coercing, anxiety, worry, frustration, anger, aggression, violence, resistance and more can pass before we finally acknowledge this.

To become conscious of doing this can save a lot of stress in our lives as we then have a choice about whether we keep trying to 'make' people do something or whether we let them pass - and, in turn, whether we have a respectful, accepting relationship with them or not.

Practising this Principle represents the difference between helping people while accepting them for who they are and how they choose to live their lives, and trying to control them and change them.

Peer Pressure

When we don't acknowledge our own right to pass we can sometimes say that we did something we didn't want to because of 'peer pressure'. This can sometimes be seen as sufficient reason for doing what we did rather than acknowledge that we had the right to pass, but for whatever reason we didn't assert that right. This means that we are likely to see ourselves as a victim of our circumstances, as if we were powerless to do any differently and so we will attribute the consequences of the action to others' influence on us rather than on our choosing to do something, even if uncomfortable with the choice.

This is a common source of unresolved conflict as our non-recognition of our right to pass leads to a sense of powerlessness about what happens in our lives and a blaming of others for our choices and actions.

It's important to note that what I am saying here is not intended as a negative judgement of our behaviours and choices and actions, it is simply an observation of what happens when we don't acknowledge our right to pass and the consequences. We do the best we can at the time in any situation we find ourselves, based on our beliefs and understandings about ourselves, the situation and the people involved in it. We may later 'wish' that we had acted differently but we didn't and the challenge is then whether we use our energy and time to reflect on the situation and go on to create better ways of dealing with similar circumstances for ourselves in the future, or we blame others for the choices we made in the past and are therefore likely to repeat those actions and choices in similar circumstances because we haven't recognised and acknowledged *that we have the right to pass* and can create alternatives for ourselves.

Acknowledging our right to pass is a recognition of our personal power in any difficult situation. Not power over others, but the power we have within ourselves to make choices, even in the face of perceived authority and influence we have ascribed to others.

> *"Everything can be taken from a man but one thing: the last of the human freedoms—to choose one's attitude in any given set of circumstances, to choose one's own way."* **Viktor E. Frankl, Man's Search for Meaning**

I have included that statement by Frankl because the point it makes is the essence of what the Principle *that we have the right to pass* is about, but also to highlight that the reference to 'man' in both the statement and the book title can symbolise a risk that we see the Principle as applying to ourselves and any group we belong to but not necessarily for those that do not belong to 'our group'.

I'm not suggesting Frankl intended it that way, he was probably simply applying the convention of the time to write with reference to the male gender in such contemplations of the human condition. But even that convention could be seen as symbolic of a tendency to see things only from our own perspective in such situations, including when asserting the right to pass.

For example, do we support our family members in practising the Principle but not our neighbours? Do we support it with others of the same race or religion as us but not those who are not? What about those of a different political view? To what extent do we try to justify the imposition of our views and expectations on others simply because of a 'difference' we see in them whether physical characteristics or in terms of their apparent values, beliefs and opinions?

Frankl does say within his statement that it is the *last of the* **human** *freedoms - to choose one's attitude in any given set of circumstances, to choose one's own way* even while referring to 'men' in other aspects of his statement and in this way it fits entirely with the Principle that we have the right to pass as it would not make sense to see it as a Principle that applies only to some and not to others.

It is our non-recognition of our right to pass, to choose our own way in any given set of circumstances and our non-recognition of others' right to do the same that obstructs the creation of effective communication and the resolution of conflict.

Many of the daily 'issues' of concern on the news, in our workplaces, within our families and communities seem to suggest that others 'make us' do something, and of course in particular circumstances it may feel that way until we have questioned that belief. While we hold on to that belief there is a sense of powerlessness associated with it, both for those of us who feel we were 'made to' do something but *also* for those who it is suggested 'made us do it' or who we see in some other way as responsible for *our* actions.

Principle 3 Challenge:

Do you allow others the right to pass?

Who do you think *should* be doing something differently?

Who is not doing something you think they *should* be doing?

Are you 'only trying to help'? Does it feel as if you are helping, or does it feel like you are wasting your time? If it feels like you are wasting your time - you probably are! And you are probably wasting their time too!

Try this:
Think about anyone you know who you have tried to help through suggestions, advice or some other action but they passed on what you offered.

1. How did you feel?
2. What do you think of them?

If your answer to 1. is *'Fine', 'No problem', 'OK'*, then that's great. But just check whether there was also a follow up to that of....

If they don't want my help, stuff 'em. Let them go and waste all their money/time/energy/career etc. - Just don't come running to me when it all messes up!

......then reflect on whether you have genuinely let them 'pass', or whether there is a resentment within you because you think they should have done what you said, or you feel they are not capable of handling things themselves and you believe your way is 'better'.

Consider the impact on *you* of this experience. Does it bring peace within you? Or is it frustration? If the latter, you are trying to control or change another. Impossible! And why would you want to?

Consider the impact on your relationship with this person. Does it lead you to feel at ease around them? Do they feel at ease around you? Or do you have some negative views about them because they didn't take up your suggestion or advice or even an unrequested 'favour' that you did for them (gave them some money, bought them a book or an item or service you think they should use etc.)?

If you are not accepting in someone their *right to pass* and hold some resentment or expectation of them that's fine, welcome to self-awareness instead of denial, welcome to recognition of your fallibilities as a human being. Just become conscious of when you are doing it and consider whether there is a more constructive way of responding, for you and for your relationship and communication with them?

I know you can find a more constructive way, because only you can. It will be unique to your situation and no prescriptions can be given here although you may create some of your own ideas with the support of this Guide.

For now, this is just about considering to what extent any non-acceptance of someone's right to pass is leading to stress or other difficulty in your life.

Just noticing will be the first step to finding a better way forward for yourself, and it is then more likely to be a better way forward for the other person(s), your relationship with them and the situation in which you previously didn't acknowledge their right to pass on your ideas and solutions 'for them'.

> *"I don't know what's best for me or you or the world. I don't try to impose my will on you or anyone else. I don't want to change you or improve you or convert you or help you or heal you. I just welcome things as they come and go. That's true love. The best way of leading people is to let them find their own way."* **Byron Katie – A Thousand Names for Joy**

That we have the right to pass

Principle 3 Notes:

Principle 4: That we do not volunteer others

This Principle relates to situations where assumptions are made about someone's willingness to do something without checking with them first. A lot of expectations and arrangements that are based on such assumptions can crumble when it emerges that the person is not willing to do what they were volunteered for. Additionally, someone who has been volunteered but has not acknowledged or felt able to assert their right to pass can feel exploited, abused, taken-for-granted, angry, resentful or any number of other difficult feelings.

When we volunteer others to do something we challenge their sense of autonomy. Sometimes it does not cause a problem as people may feel happy to go along with something they have been volunteered for, but it is unlikely they will accept this happening on a frequent basis.

For example, difficulties can arise in a workplace[11] when bosses expect employees to do more than their job description specifies. People have implicitly volunteered themselves to do what is in their job description they agree to when they start, but when they are expected to do more than the description says on

---

11 www.communicationandconflict.com/workplace.html

a frequent basis, apparently without the choice to say 'No', resistance is likely to arise and destructive responses to the situation can follow.

People will 'go the extra mile' in the workplace when they feel safe that they have a choice whether to do more than their job description states or not.

If someone in a workplace believes they have been volunteered to do something but that their views were not considered, they may, in time, start to act in the way described as 'jobsworth' - sticking rigidly to the details of their job description in order to protect themselves from a further sense of exploitation.

Another phenomenon that can arise in situations of volunteering others is to use comments such as '*You are not being a team player*' - emotionally blackmailing the person to persuade them to do as they were volunteered.

This is an ineffective approach to management, co-working, and any relationship as it is seeking to impose an expectation of being volunteered rather than drawing upon someone's enthusiasm or willingness to do something, which is more effectively achieved by asking for offers than by volunteering people.

In an environment where the right to pass is recognised a healthy working environment is likely to exist. But where asserting the right to pass is seen as *being difficult* or when people experience emotional blackmail or 'guilt tripping' to try to get them to take on something they didn't volunteer for, or are led to believe there may be other consequences that feel threatening to them, it is unlikely that a healthy working relationship exists. In such circumstances it is inevitable that the work environment will not be as productive and creative as it could be.

And of course, volunteering others can have damaging consequences in other areas of human interaction such as in the family, between partners, in formal meetings, amongst social groups etc.

Consider the following questions:

- How often do you presume that someone will be ok with doing something you have volunteered them for without checking with them?

- How often does it lead to a problem with them?

- How often do you describe other people - employees, partners, children, friends etc. as 'difficult' or 'stubborn' or

'unreasonable' when they don't do what you have
volunteered them to do without consultation?

- How often do you stop to look at *yourself* and how you
  have acted when this happens?

If you do volunteer others, do you continue to justify your
reasons for doing so with thoughts such as:

*They should do it! I don't care if it's not in their job description.
I'm their boss they should do as I say.*

They should call me more often, I'm their partner.

*They should want to go and stay with their grandparents, it's
only a silly football match they are missing. And I am their parent
after all, they should do as I tell them!*

The important question is: **Did your volunteering others lead
to a conflict to which the responses have become
destructive?**

Many of us will recognise these events happening in our lives
and as well, perhaps, the difficulties arising from them. When
such things occur, we can choose to look at ourselves and find a
better way of *inviting* or requesting that people do something,
while also acknowledging their right to pass.

Alternatively, we can 'point the finger outwards' and blame others for the problem that arises and experience progressive resistance, disconnection and relationship breakdown. We may use words to describe those who are 'proving difficult' by saying *they are apathetic, they don't care, they are lazy, too easy-going, need a kick up the*.....

You get the picture!

Even where we manage to volunteer others and overcome the resistance, perhaps through veiled threats or emotional blackmail, or 'senior rank', the disconnection and relationship breakdown will still follow. These consequences may show themselves at a later time when the individual's resistance is harder to overcome and they are more confident about asserting their autonomy, or circumstances have changed such that the other person cannot be so easily 'volunteered' without their consent.

> *Dictators ride to and fro upon tigers which they dare not dismount. And the tigers are getting hungry!* - **Winston Churchill**

This is perhaps a good time to re-emphasise that the Principles are not 'rules'! This isn't a book about political correctness in speech. The Principles are designed to help you develop a mindfulness about your communication, to look at your intention in what you say and to consider the potential consequences of your communication practice so that you can 'own' and accept those consequences rather than be surprised by them.

Here's an example:

You may be a parent who is having difficulty with a teenage daughter. She's just starting to become a bit more independent and while you've been used to giving her 'good advice' and telling her how to deal with one thing or another as she grew up, she's now becoming angry when you try to bestow your adult wisdom upon her.

The Principle *that we do not volunteer others* has relevance here and supporting the development of an *adult-adult relationship*[12] can be assisted through practices common to mediation and conflict coaching such as using open questions and not closed, leading questions or suggestions[13].

Open questions such as:

- *What do you think?*
- *What would you like?*
- *How could you do that?*

---

[12] www.communicationandconflict.com/Adult-Adult.html
[13] www.communicationandconflict.com/questioning.html

.....allow and support creation of the choice of action to come from the person being asked. This is in contrast to veiled suggestions and 'sage advice' appearing as closed questions such as *'Could you..?'* or *'Have you tried....?'* or *'Don't you think it would be better to....?'* or 'directives' such as *'You must/must not....'* or *'You should/shouldn't...'*.

Sometimes people scoff at the liberty afforded by a 'creative questioning' approach with teenagers or even younger children, but with an emerging adult that liberty will become more and more available as she matures and standing in its way is likely to cause a distancing rather than a closeness in the relationship between parents and their children.

In such a situation a teenage daughter may start to keep secrets from and deceive her parents if they try to constrain her and impose their views, in order to take the freedom she sees as already hers. The use of open questions to help her make her own decisions means there is nothing for her to oppose, resent or resist, as nothing is being imposed. This approach would nurture her development as a maturing adult in that it encourages her to form her own views and ideas about herself and how she should act.

She is more likely to trust her parents because they are not trying to constrain or control her, and they are more likely to trust her as they see her develop the capacity to create her own way in the world with the encouragement and support of their open questions.

And, just to be clear, the example applies to all parent-teenager relationships, whatever their gender identity!

Similar situations occur in other relationships. The *dominated* wife, the *henpecked* husband, the *bullied* brother, the *overworked* helper are all situations that arise when someone is continually volunteered to do things that they feel they have not been given a choice in.

In all such situations a more exploratory, invitational approach to creating communication through the use of open questions is much more likely to lead to a closer, co-operative, trusting relationship than one that is tinged with resistance and resentment.

Of course, anyone can refuse to do what they have been volunteered to do – they have the right to pass - but the impact on the relationship between people when one is volunteering the other(s) can be damaging because of the difficult feelings that arise and the attempts to avoid the one who volunteers or, if they can't be avoided, an angry outburst of frustration.

So, in recognition of the potential risks of using a directive, volunteering approach to your communication with people consider the following:

- How often do you volunteer others?

- Do you feel that you 'have' to, to get them to do things?

- Does it become more and more difficult to 'get them to do something'?

- Are you at risk of being labelled a 'bully' or some other negative label for your frequent volunteering of another?

- Do you see those you volunteer as apathetic or uncooperative?

If you said yes to any or all of the above, then there are, of course, other options:

- Not volunteering others, but open invitation with the acceptance of the *right to pass.*

- Reflecting on whether your approach to trying to ensure someone does what you have volunteered them to do could be seen as emotional blackmail, guilt-tripping, intimidating or manipulative, even if not your intention.

- Creating an approach which is based on requests for co-operation.

- If seeking to support someone or help them with a difficulty they are experiencing, reflecting on whether you are 'taking over' their situation and trying to 'rescue' them rather than helping them to create their own answers through enquiry, interest and curiosity using open questions.

And why would we choose those options? Not because they are 'morally correct' - who can decide that? - but because it works better *for us* when we replace volunteering others with requests and invitations and respect for their autonomy!

But what if *we* are the person being volunteered and the other person frequently tries to volunteer us for things?

Well, to remind you of Principle 3:

We always have a choice. We have the right to pass!

But do we recognise it and acknowledge it and then make our decision whether to agree to do what we have been volunteered to do - or do we convince ourselves we don't have a choice by not acknowledging our *right to pass*?

If we convince ourselves we don't have a choice, we are abdicating responsibility for our situation. We are not taking ownership[14] of our responses and actions. And so, our 'being volunteered' is likely to continue.

If we recognise that we have a choice, do we address our discontent at being volunteered with the person who did it?

If we don't, and we may not wish to, then we can accept the situation but still seek to support ourselves as effectively as possible within it. Sometimes we'd rather accept it than challenge it, and that's fine. *We have the right to pass* on that as well. It's our choice. Or we may decide that being volunteered to do something just once doesn't matter but if it happens more than 3 times perhaps, we will address it with the other person. In doing so *we* are accepting the situation as we can't expect the person volunteering us to know by telepathy that we are unhappy about being volunteered.

What we need to watch out for however is whether we tell ourselves, and, possibly, others as well:

'They made me do it!' - when they didn't, or *'I had to do it!'* – when you didn't.

---

14 www.communicationandconflict.com/ownership.html

When we tell ourselves this we create a 'victim' status for ourselves, and put ourselves in the disempowered[15] position of waiting for the person who volunteered us to change.

While we wait, passive in our expectation of change in things we can't control, we are not acknowledging our capacity *to create the change* we need. For example:

- By removing ourselves from the situation and the consequences of the other's actions.

- By communicating that we don't wish to do the thing we are being volunteered for.

- By focusing on creating ways of supporting ourselves more effectively in the situation if we don't feel we can change our external circumstances.

All of these active options change our status from being a victim to being someone who 'owns' their decisions and actions – as well as their consequences.

Again, this is an observation of what can happen in unresolved conflict situations and how the way we communicate can help

---

[15] www.communicationandconflict.com/empowerment.html

or hinder the resolution of that situation. It is not a criticism of anyone who has found themselves in that situation of feeling powerless and a victim in the past or presently. It is an experience we are all likely to have had at some points in our lives.

Developing a mindfulness about the situations where we have been volunteered to do something but we have not, at the time, recognised our *right to pass,* or not felt able to assert it, can help us to see whether we have hoped in desperation for things we can't control to change or whether we have been able to look to ourselves to create change in the things we *can* control.

We can become so focused outwardly on the people who have 'made us' do things while impotently wishing they didn't that we overlook the power we have to change our circumstances in any given situation.

Through developing an awareness of this, a mindfulness about our responses, we can start to re-establish our power in such situations rather than remain stuck in a place of victimhood.

It is often interesting to me in mediation and conflict coaching cases that I am involved in how often it is the case that someone has not ever considered the possibility that they could decide not to do something they have been volunteered to do, whether

91

in work situations or in family, community and other social contexts.

Once reflected on and recognised, consideration of how they can go about declining their involvement in the task or expectation they have been volunteered for can follow. Often, in joint mediation meetings where someone communicates this to the other person they've had a difficulty with they are surprised to find that the person who has volunteered them had not realised the extent to which it was difficult or upsetting for them.

In situations where there has not been an opportunity to address it directly with the person it is still the case that they are able to consider how they can do so in future similar situations, this time without the unquestioned belief that they have to do what they have been volunteered to do.

There are connections between all of the Principles which you will come to identify the more you consider them and put them into practice but the connections between Principles 3, 4 and 5 are particularly evident because they deal with the extent to which we are able to recognise and 'own' our decisions, actions, behaviours, perspectives and power in different situations as well as the consequences and responsibilities that follow from doing so.

Principle 4 Challenge:

I was on the train the other day and the woman opposite me was talking to someone on her mobile phone:

'Tell Terry to come and pick you up from the station.'

'Yeah, Terry can come and pick you up, give him a call.'

I wondered how Terry would feel about being volunteered to pick her friend up. Simply by changing the wording from 'Tell Terry.... ' or 'Terry can....' to 'Ask Terry if he can...' the whole nature of the interaction would be different. Ownership of the action is still Terry's in the latter statement while in the former statements he is not acknowledged as having a choice. He has been volunteered.

Terry might not have minded being volunteered. But he might. It could easily be a source of accumulated resentment that he is frequently being volunteered to drive people around and pick them up. What has he done about it?

Consider your language during the next few days. Do you ever use similar language to the above, about someone you know, to volunteer them?

Consider these questions as well:

- Do you have a 'Terry' in your life?

- Are you sometimes treated in the same way as Terry? You may not mind if it is not very often. You may tell yourself: *'It's sort of part of the give and take of getting on with people'.* Perhaps? Or does it happen more often than you are happy with? What would help you to address that?

- Do you volunteer someone on a regular basis? Are you sure they don't mind?

- Why do you volunteer them rather than ask them?

Again, just try to notice your answers to these questions and the extent to which they may have relevance to your relationships with others, particularly where you are presently experiencing some kind of difficulty.

That we do not volunteer others

Principle 4 Notes:

Principle 5: That we speak only for ourselves and speak in the 'I' using I-statements

*There are many reasons given for **'speaking in the 'I' by using I-statements'** but one reason that is not often noted is that to speak in the 'I' is actually a more accurate communication of something we think or feel than to do otherwise.*

When we speak for others as if they agree with us, we are saying something that is either not true or not verifiable:

- *We all want to be wealthy.*
- *Everyone knows that she is a difficult person to get along with.*
- *No-one would want to live around here.*
- *Everyone can see this country is in moral decline!*

When we speak as if a subjective view is a fact, it often is not:

- *They are only saying that because they are racist!*
- *British children are the unhappiest in the world!*
- *Crime in London is a constant threat!*
- *That was a hurtful comment!*

When we speak in the 'I' using I-statements we are saying what *we know to be true as it is **our own** thoughts and feelings* we are expressing:

- *I would like to be wealthy / Being wealthy isn't particularly important to me.*
- *I find her difficult to get along with / I get on with her just fine.*
- *I wouldn't want to live around here / I would like to live around here.*
- *I'm upset by some of the things I see happen in our country / I think our country is a great place to live.*

....and when we acknowledge our view is subjective rather than a fact:

- *I think they have said that because I'm a different race to them / I don't think my race is the reason they have said that.*
- *I feel sad that there are children in this country who say they are unhappy / I met some children today who said how much they love living in this country.*
- *When I'm in London I often worry about being the victim of crime / I've never really felt vulnerable to crime while living in London.*
- *I found that comment hurtful / I didn't feel hurt by that comment.*

Note that you may have your own preferred ways of restating the above using I-statements. The versions I have given are possible alternatives, but not the only ones. As I-statements however, they are all more accurate and more effective forms of communication about the topic concerned than the original statements for the reasons given.

The conscious use of I-statements means that we are less likely to speak for others. We don't presume to know what they think and feel or why they have said or done something.

To speak for others is a major inhibitor to communicating effectively as those who do not agree with what we have said on their behalf can feel as if their views have not been considered. This leads to the risk that they will 'switch off' from us and become distant and it is in this way that a relationship and communication breakdown begins to occur.

Alternatively, they may become actively resistant to what we are saying and less inclined to co-operate with us. We risk losing someone's trust if we have spoken for them and misrepresented how they feel and what they think. After all, if we've done it once, when else might we do it? What else might be said 'on their behalf' which misrepresents their views?

Speaking for others is a very common and ineffective communication practice. It may be that we do it to 'reassure ourselves' that our view is widely or even unanimously held by others, or in order to try to convince others that our view is 'right' and 'absolutely true' for everyone rather than just subjectively true for us.

To acknowledge that our view of the world is not a 'fact' can be quite uncomfortable and so we may avoid the use of an I-statement because it feels less threatening, even though avoiding its use leads to a less accurate statement and therefore creates less effective communication and a greater likelihood of a relationship difficulty with those we have spoken for.

The use of I-statements means we are stating *our own* view and 'putting it out there' as a statement of *our* thoughts and feelings about an issue while remaining open to hearing others' views on the issue.

When we are mindful of this way of communicating it means we can also hear others' views as being their own and not facts even if they don't use I-statements to express themselves.

When we recognise this, it helps us to avoid getting caught up in arguments with others in which we speak as if we are expressing contradictory 'facts' about something which cannot be intrinsically factual. Instead we can see that they have a view that differs from ours but neither is absolutely 'right'. Their view is subjectively right for them and our view is subjectively right for us. This allows us to listen more effectively to what others are saying with a view to trying to understand their perspective rather than focus on our 'defence' of our view if it differs from theirs as if one must be the absolutely 'right' view and so, by default any other view is 'wrong'.

The recognition of the subjectivity of our viewpoint is a pivotal feature of any resolved conflict and is one of the many reasons why I-statements are so often considered important contributors to effective communication and the resolution of conflict.

Speaking for others is like riding roughshod over alternative views and will inevitably, however 'powerful' we are, and on whatever issue it is we are speaking, lead to resistance to what we are saying.

Implicit within the practice of speaking for others is the suggestion that we don't have to listen to their views because we 'know them already'.

When you see the significance of using I-statements you will notice that some politicians, journalists, campaigners and activists will use ineffective communication about very serious issues because their focus remains on a *subjective* view being defended or portrayed as *objectively true or correct*. This, in turn, leads to a dismissive stance towards others' perspectives rather than remain open to listening to them. As a consequence, the discussion becomes one of attack and defend rather than the pursuit of learning, change and growth.

But it is not only politicians, campaigners, journalists and activists who are prone to doing this. Any one of us is likely to speak for others at different times in our communication. What matters for creating effective communication is whether we recognise it is what we are doing, whether we can be mindful of doing so.

If we have no recognition of this ineffective communication practice we are very likely to be continuously locked in battles with others in the belief that we always have to 'win' our arguments by destroying the arguments of others. Recognising that our views and theirs are subjective does not mean we let go of our views or give them up, it means that we can work towards a situation that accommodates both views and moves towards resolution of the conflict *situation* rather than pursue a path of mutual destruction of each other as *people* whether verbally or sometimes more tragically, physically as well.

The aim of an argument or discussion should not be victory but progress. – Joseph Joubert

Principle 5 Challenge:

Consider your language during the next few days and try to observe:

How often do you make a statement as if it is a fact, when really it is just your opinion, or an unverifiable generalisation?

Try to note it down or at least remember it and later on, try making an I-statement based on your original statement. How does it feel to say it as an I-statement?

Try practising the use of I-statements with others and see if you notice any differences in how they respond to you. Look back at the examples given at the start of this Principle section if you need help in creating them. Keep them simple. Sometimes I-statements are portrayed as being quite complex and long winded and almost 'scripted' but they don't have to be. For example:

Rainy weather is miserable!

> *I feel miserable when it's raining/ I enjoy the rain.*

You are such an unreasonable person!

> *...what you are suggesting doesn't work for me.*

While the last statement is not strictly an I-statement, it is still an example of someone speaking for themselves, expressing a subjective view about a suggestion that has been made by another person and not a 'statement of objective fact' about the person who made it - as the preceding phrase implies (*You are...unreasonable*).

Listen to others' statements and see if you notice a difference in your own response when someone uses an I-statement and when you hear someone use a 'you' statement or makes a subjective generalisation or assumption but states it as if it is an objective fact.

Just notice the impact of practising this Principle, or not. Developing a mindfulness about this will assist you in creating more effective communication with others and help you resolve conflicts more creatively and effectively.

That we speak only for ourselves and speak in the 'I' using I-statements

Principle 5 Notes:

Principle 6: That we speak, but not too often or for too long

When someone is perceived to be speaking too often or for too long by a listener, the threat to effective communication and conflict resolution arises because there seems to be no opportunity for learning, discussion or relationship building. The interaction feels as if it is 'one-way' and so there isn't a sense in which mutual and shared communication is being created.

A listener could be one other person or they could be one of many listeners in a meeting or group. As more 'air time' is taken up, the listener's interest in what the speaker is saying can wane and sometimes even turn to resentment towards them for taking up so much time if the listener also wants to speak.

Boredom can arise in someone who feels they already know what the speaker is saying or are not interested in what they have to say. And of course, various other inhibiting responses can occur that replace the interest and engagement that normally takes place in the creation of effective communication if there is a perception that someone is speaking too often or for too long.

However, there is a risk that we treat this (subjective) perception as an objective fact - different listeners will have different views of whether a speaker *is* speaking too often or for too long. Some may want to hear more!

It can be easy to belittle someone who speaks more than we would like with comments such as '*They just like the sound of their own voice*' etc. but ultimately this doesn't change anything. Instead it entrenches us in our frustration or resentment and, if we want the situation to change, is not practising the first Principle *that we treat each other with respect* in a way that would start to support that change. So ultimately, *we* also lose out if we do this. Nothing changes and a difficulty continues or escalates.

Applying Principle 5 – *that we speak only for ourselves and speak in the 'I' using I-statements* would enable us to be more accurate and to contribute more effectively in our communication about our perception of this kind of experience:

Do we say:

*This speaker **is** boring/long winded/verbose etc.*

or

I find this speaker to be boring/long winded/verbose etc.?

Better still, as you will see when you read about Principle 7, we can say:

I find what this speaker is saying to be boring/long winded/verbose etc.

When we acknowledge that the perception of someone speaking too often or for too long is our own subjective view and not a 'fact', a lot can be done by both the listener and the speaker to improve the quality of communication created in such situations.

The skills of *Listening, Summarising and Questioning*[16] can be useful for both the listener and speaker in maximising the effectiveness of communication in a situation where a speaker is perceived to be speaking too often or for too long.

What the Listener can do:
People sometimes speak more often than they need to, or for longer than they need to about something when they are not sure they have been understood.

Summarising[17] what the speaker has said (in the way previously described for Co-listening in the section on Principle 2) identifies

---

[16] www.communicationandconflict.com/skills.html
[17] www.communicationandconflict.com/summarising.html

clearly to them that they have been heard, which means they are less likely to repeat themselves.

Summarising also allows the speaker to hear back what they have said, enabling them to 'hear themselves' in their own words - if the summary is an effective one - and this can enable them to understand themselves better and perhaps gain new insights into what it is they are saying.

This is an important benefit for the speaker as sometimes people will talk at length about a topic because they are trying to 'get their head round it', and are, indeed, *looking for interaction* in order to help them crystallise or consolidate their ideas.

However, we can never actually know the reasons why someone, in our view, speaks too often or for too long and, in many ways, it doesn't matter why.

Whatever the reason, and because it is just our perception anyway, summarising what someone has said provides an effective way of helping the situation to become a discussion and through the interaction that ensues, effective communication can be created rather than a monologue.

Questioning

Further to summarising, another practice that can reduce the impact of our perception that someone is speaking too often or for too long is to use questioning[18] skills to encourage further understanding and expression of what they have to say. This may seem counterintuitive as it would seem to stimulate more talking, but it serves the following purposes:

- For someone who is speaking at length because they aren't sure their message is getting through, a question shows genuine interest (and the questions do have to be genuine, from a place of curiosity and interest, if you wish to create effective communication) and reassures them of this. As a consequence, it is more likely they will move on, satisfied that they haven't 'lost' their audience.

- In someone who is speaking because they want to understand their own thoughts and feelings on a topic, a question creates the opportunity for rethinking the topic in order to give an answer, which can help the speaker to gain new insights and move on.

- Asking questions also means that there is an interaction rather than a monologue which will always increase the opportunity to create better communication and is therefore less likely to feel as if someone is speaking too often or for too long.

---

18 www.communicationandconflict.com/questioning.html

Sometimes, however, the perception of another speaking too often or for too long is because we want to speak just as often and for just as long and so we develop a sense of 'competition' or even resentment that someone has 'got there first', or seems to be given a 'privileged platform'.

In such cases it is likely that the creation of effective communication, between ourselves and others is not our focus but simply to feel heard, irrespective of whether our contribution relates or responds to what the speaker is saying. As a consequence, what occurs will be two parallel monologues that do not come together to form any kind of effective communication.

What we overlook when this happens is that *it is by engaging with the speaker* through listening, summarising and questioning in the ways described, *that we maximise our own opportunity to be heard.*

It is always interesting to me that when a group which holds meetings together of some kind but have come to a situation of difficulty and communication breakdown, it is almost always the case that the nature of their communication is a continuous 'spear fight' of competing monologues with opinions flying back and forth and little listening to, or interest in understanding each other's points of view. Accusations that others are speaking too often or for too long, even if not phrased in that way, are frequent in such situations. The introduction of open questions to replace 'opinions' and which indicate interest in and receptivity to others' views can have an immediate, significant impact on the nature of the meetings and their effectiveness as an opportunity for communicating.

Some meetings continue in 'spear fighting' mode for long periods of time, sometimes years, and as a consequence feel heavy and boring and ineffective, and often more derogatory phrases are used to describe them, often alongside criticisms of particular attendees who are seen as the cause of the ineffectiveness. But anyone can ask an open question instead of continue to give opinions, and if the question's purpose is to learn more about others' perspectives and not to try to 'catch them out', it can immediately increase the effectiveness of the communication created by all who attend the meeting.

A further challenge that can obstruct the improvement of such meetings is a further exchange of opinions about *who should ask the open questions!* Some volunteer the Chair of the meeting to ask them and so we see Principle 4 not being applied and the meeting remains stuck, while sometimes attendees speak for themselves (applying Principle 5 even if not aware that they are) and go on to ask the open questions that support connection and the creation of effective communication towards a shared purpose of creativity and resolution of conflict.

When we are the speaker

If we see ourselves as someone who tends to speak too often or for too long, we can use the same skills of listening, summarising and questioning, but applied in a different way to optimise our contribution to the creation of effective communication.

Summarising what we have said from time to time gives people a breather and time to stop and reflect. All listeners can miss something that a speaker says and the number of things missed will grow and grow as a speaker continues without pause. As it grows and grows the audience can feel less and less connected to what we are saying and so occasional summaries will help to prevent this.

Questions also improve the communication we create by inviting engagement from our audience, whether that is just one person or hundreds. It also gives us a feel for our listeners' interests as well as the 'change of tune' that hearing another person's voice can bring to keeping the communication dynamic.

However, if speaking to a large group, just taking questions from the audience can become stagnant at times if we have others who are also perceived to speak too often or for too long in asking their questions. To reduce this, we can ask the audience to form groups and bring their group's question(s) to the discussion. In this way we are also promoting communication and engagement *between* our listeners – and furthermore, *we are speaking, but not too often or for too long.*

I have a personal discomfort in attending conferences with 'keynote speakers' where there can be hundreds of people passively sat in a room while just one person speaks at length on a particular topic. Even where such topics are of interest to me I still feel there has been a wasted opportunity for interactive communication and learning because the audience has not been involved. It is very unlikely that the speaker is the only person with knowledge and experience in relation to the topic being presented and while the presentation remains a monologue they are missing the opportunity to learn from those in their audience, through hearing their different perspectives or deeper insights about the topic.

As a consequence, I rarely attend conferences, and if asked to give a presentation or keynote address I always advise the conference organiser that it will be an interactive session so that those present can have the opportunity to communicate amongst each other and with me about the presentation theme requested.

Principle 6 Challenge:

The next time you believe that someone is speaking too often or for too long, ask yourself the following:

- Am I still listening to what they are saying?

- Would a summary from them help me to keep in touch with what they are trying to convey?

- Could *I* give that summary? *Remember, a summary is not a test, it is a means through which you can work together with the speaker to ensure that the communication between you, and your mutual understanding of what is being discussed, is optimised.*

- If not a summary, what open question could I ask to help the speaker complete their commentary or explanation which will also help me to feel engaged in what they are saying? It doesn't have to be a 'clever' question, just one that genuinely seeks to explore some aspect of what the speaker is saying to a greater depth.

Why am I here?
But there is another challenge in relation to this Principle, one that asks you to take responsibility for finding yourself in a situation where you consider others to be speaking for too

often or for too long.If you are in a place where little that is being discussed is of interest to you and you find the meeting to be a waste of your time, the question has to be asked of you:

Why have you put yourself in that situation in the first place?

Effective communication is not about saying you 'should' be interested in everything anyone ever says.

Remember Principle 3? You have the right to pass!

The Principle that we speak but not too often or for too long is in relation to maximising the effectiveness of our communication about something we *want* to communicate about.

Others present may be very interested in what is being discussed, or they may not, they can speak for themselves on that matter. If you find yourself in a meeting where you feel someone is speaking too often or for too long and the topic is not of interest to you, the problem is not their desire to discuss the topic at length and with great frequency, it is your placing yourself in a situation where what is being discussed is not of interest to you.

Why are you there?

And if you can't find an acceptable answer to that question, what will you do to remove yourself?

Be wary of telling yourself *'I have to be at the meeting, my job requires it of me!'*

Really?

If you are to do your job to the best of your ability and your manager wants you to be as effective as possible, is it effective to be in meetings that are of no relevance or serve no purpose for you?

What communication have you had with the person you feel might 'expect' you to attend? If none then you are speaking for them and assuming that it is so. And if you are telling yourself you have to attend due to a sense of peer pressure or social expectation, what has meant you are unable to assert your right to pass?

And of course, the same applies in other contexts such as social gatherings, family gatherings, community events etc. If you feel people speak too often or for too long at those meetings and you are not interested enough in what is being discussed to try to engage with the speakers in the ways described above, then why are you attending the meeting anyway?

When we acknowledge such things within ourselves we can, again, move ourselves out of our 'victim' status to one of actively creating our own choices and actions and thus reduce the likelihood of remaining in a repeated, unresolved conflict situation arising from our perception that someone is speaking too often or for too long.

Principle 6 Notes

Principle 7: That we challenge the behaviour and not the person

Being aware of this Principle enables us to see others as individual human beings who change in their behaviour and thoughts and actions on a continuous basis. It allows us to see the uniqueness of each person and how they can grow and change and struggle and evolve.

When we don't practise this Principle, it can lead us to put up barriers to others by labelling *them* on the basis of a snap-shot judgement we have made as a result of observing a particular behaviour we subjectively perceive them to have exhibited. It denies the possibility of them ever being other than the judgement and subsequent label[19] we apply when in reality all of us act differently at different times in different contexts.

I might be considered 'lazy' when it comes to housework, but that may be because someone has seen my place when there are unwashed dishes in the sink and a few crumbs on the carpet.

---

[19] www.communicationandconflict.com/labels.html

They may not know that I have just recovered from an illness or have been looking after a sick relative and I've considered housework temporarily less important.

The label applied as a result of a momentary, subjective observation of a behaviour or situation becomes a description of 'Alan' *as a person*, and is then easily assumed to extend to other areas of my life.

Once the label has been applied the labeller will notice other actions that seem to reinforce their belief in their label for me and overlook those that contradict it.

This is the basis of all stereotyping, prejudice and discrimination.

If other people who have not been ascribed a particular label behave in the same way, their behaviours will be overlooked as the observer is not looking to reinforce their belief about those other people.

This is a common practice in communication. Sometimes professionals apply a label to their clients without considering the validity of the label and the damage it can cause to the relationship with the client:

- The *lazy* or *stupid* pupil,
- The *dysfunctional* family

- The *depressive* patient
- The *mentally ill* tenant etc.

All of us are prone to applying labels to others on the basis of observing a behaviour and generalising the label for that behaviour to the person who exhibits it and, often, on to the group we see them as being a member of.

- My boss *is* a *bully,*
- My partner *is boring,*
- John in Accounts *is manipulative,*
- Black people *are criminals,*
- Men *are violent*
- Muslims *are terrorists*
- The Police *are racist*..... etc.

All of the above label the person (or group of people!) and not their momentary, subjectively interpreted behaviour.

The labeller does not consider or acknowledge that the person labelled will act entirely differently in other circumstances, as all of us do, nor are they likely to acknowledge that their observation of a behaviour was their subjective interpretation of a momentary event and not an objectively true and permanent fact.

Sometimes a behaviour seen in a person who belongs to a particular group is not just generalised to that person but to all people who are seen as 'like' them – those who are believed to belong to the same group. This is the basis for broad, societal breakdowns in communication and consequent conflict, not just at the level of individual, personal relationships.

Consider the following scenario:
You are unfortunately assaulted by another person. You would describe them as 'white', however you may also describe them as 'male' and you may also describe them as Muslim. If you do not practise this Principle you may go on to challenge the person and not the behaviour and apply labels such as:

- *'Men are violent – I got attacked by one the other day'*
- *'White people are violent – one just came up to me and hit me the other day!'*
- *'Muslims* are violent! *– I was walking along the road the other day and one just assaulted me as I passed them'.*

Of course, none of those generalisations are accurate, but different people may, as a consequence of their past experiences, what they hear on the news, what their family or friends have told them, what politicians, celebrities, campaigners, others say etc., choose to associate one of those personal characteristics with violence.

The only truth in the matter is that the person who was violent....*was violent*....in that moment. Their gender, their skin colour and their religion are irrelevant to the behaviour they exhibited, but when we challenge the person (or group we selectively identify them as belonging to) and not the behaviour we create ineffective communication because it suggests that the gender, skin colour, religion, age, size, sexuality etc. was *the causal factor* in what happened.

One approach leads to a belief that *'they were male, and that's the reason why they were violent'*, while the other accurately recounts that they were violent and coincidentally and irrelevantly happened to be white, Muslim, male, from England, tall, dark-haired, right-handed, gay, young etc.

An awareness of, and commitment to the Principle *that we challenge the behaviour and not the person* helps us to reflect on any labels we apply to others and gain a recognition that we have, or believe we have observed a momentary or 'one-off' incidence of the behaviour and that our label for that behaviour is not a continuously exhibited characteristic of the person (or of a group we see the person as 'belonging' to).

We may find it difficult to let go of the label we have for someone, even if it is a 'positive' label, but ultimately it will always be a label *we* have subjectively applied (and so is not a 'fact'), and then sought to reinforce by selectively observing and interpreting their behaviours to fit with our label, rather than a recognition that someone's behaviours will continually vary.

Compare the following statements that might be made by a teacher to a pupil:

Jamie, you haven't done your homework again. I think your parents will need to know how lazy you are. I'll be writing home to them about this.

Ok, Jamie, this is the second time you haven't handed in your homework. What's stopping you from being able to do this? What would help you to be able to do it?

The first example simply dismisses the child with a label *(lazy)* and does not seek to support him in changing the situation, nor does it place any expectation on him to do so, nor implies any belief that he *can* change. The comment about his parents suggests a 'report' about him being 'lazy' to fix the label permanently 'in writing'.

The second example begins a dialogue about his *behaviour* and what has happened to try to understand the reasons behind the pupil's lack of homework and places the onus on him to work with the teacher to create a way forward in improving the situation. No label is necessary as it serves no purpose in addressing the situation. It is also far less likely to receive resistance arising from rejection of the label and resentment because of its application. Practising the Principle in this way supports the creation of effective communication about the homework issue and enables change and growth through the conflict that exists in relation to it.

The use of labelling to challenge the person and not the behaviour is extremely common in day to day communication, but as is the case for many of the Principles, *to challenge the behaviour and not the person* is a more accurate statement about a situation than to do otherwise. No one 'is lazy' all the time, but *their behaviour* may be (subjectively) perceived to be so, some of the time.

Besides, or perhaps because of the greater accuracy when communicating, applying the Principle *that we challenge (or comment) on the behaviour not the person* is more likely to be received openly by someone than a negative statement about *them*, as if that is fundamentally *what they are!* Labelling a person leaves no room for change or review, because there is no acknowledgement of the capacity for change, nor that the person may be different in other situations.

The phenomenon of 'demonising' someone when in a dispute with them is manifested through labelling the person and not their behaviour and serves no effective purpose in supporting the resolution of conflict as well as being an inaccurate and therefore ineffective contribution to communication.

Challenging someone's behaviour does allow for review of the behaviour and the possibility of change and does not diminish the person to one simple negative, and possibly derogatory label. It also intrinsically acknowledges the subjectivity of the perception of the behaviour and accommodates the possibility for it to be reinterpreted when raised for review and discussion. Labelling a person or group suggests an 'objective truth' about them and so does not invite any exploration or possibility of reinterpretation.

The challenging of people through the use of labels, and not their behaviour, will almost always be present in situations where a conflict has remained unresolved or has escalated.

If we wish to be listened to by someone who has done something we are concerned about we are more likely to achieve this if we speak of *what they have done* that concerns us rather than simply label *them*. Labelling someone is likely to lead to defensiveness and possibly a retaliatory label in reply to us and not discussion of the action or behaviour we are concerned about.

Developing a mindfulness about our use of this Principle within our communication can make a significant impact on the likelihood of a difficult situation being resolved, as well as make it much less likely that the situation will become 'difficult' in the first place.

My boss is a bully!

When I provide mediation and a client uses a statement about another person, for example that *'they are a bully'*, I will always explore such a statement with a question such as:

'What is it that X has done that leads you to say that about them?'

That very simple question can support a more effective and constructive discussion about an allegation that someone is a bully (which is rarely, if ever, possible to prove) because it supports a discussion about the behaviours, actions and communications that have occurred in the situation. Once described, they can then be discussed, reflected on and resolved through the creation of different ways of responding in future, whether more self-supporting actions and behaviours by the person who feels bullied, or by the person accused of bullying who almost always has not recognised how their behaviours have been experienced by the other person.

The same exploratory question can be used in relation to any label such as *they are arrogant, they are rude, they are inconsiderate, unreasonable, stupid, an idiot* etc.

When discussions involve a person-not-behaviour 'tennis match' of labels *(You're a bully - You're too sensitive)* it goes nowhere because it becomes an entrenched, stressful and personal attack/defend argument and ultimately destroys the relationship.

Focusing on exploration and discussion of the behaviour and not on labelling the person supports the possibilities for a relationship to be re-established on a more considered, conscious, mindful basis and this is how such practices as mediation and conflict coaching support constructive change and growth through conflict because their sole purpose is to assist with that happening.

But what if I want to use 'nice labels'?
As an interesting flip-side to the application of this Principle, it is also important to bear it in mind when we make positive comments about others. Consider the following statement:

'Jilly, that project plan you produced for the Senior Management Team was so useful in helping us to create a strategy for this upcoming contract bid. It really outlined the possibilities and the things we need to be cautious of that we could easily have overlooked. Thanks.'

This is a much more useful, informative and effective communication of praise than:

'Jilly, that project plan was great, you are amazing! Thanks!'

And here's another example:

'Sanjay, thank you for helping me to clear up after our painting and crafts session, it means we can now go out a lot sooner for our visit to the park.'

This is much more informative than:

'Sanjay, you are such a good little boy'.

Remember, the Principles are not rules! You may enjoy giving someone a nice, positive label and this isn't saying you should stop. However, consider when the person does something that doesn't fit your positive label. Do you give them a new label that contradicts the previous one? If so, which one do they believe?

I'm just asking!

Practising this Principle supports the creation of more effective communication because it gives clearer, more useful detail about an issue than is contained in a label. It supports the resolution of conflict because it leads to a focus on the real problem - the actions, behaviours and communications that have occurred within the difficult situation so that these can be reflected on and changed. Practising this Principle also helps to redirect the focus of attention and energy away from *personal* attacks and defence and towards resolution of the *problem.*

"Hate the sin and not the sinner is a precept which, though easy enough to understand, is rarely practiced, and that is why the poison of hatred spreads in the world... It is quite proper to resist and attack a system, but to resist and attack its author is tantamount to resisting and attacking oneself, for we are all tarred with the same brush, and are children of one and the same Creator, and as such the divine powers within us are infinite. To slight a single human being is to slight those divine powers, and thus to harm not only that being but with him the whole world." - **Mahatma Gandhi, The Story of My Experiments With Truth**

Principle 7 Challenge:

Consider a situation where someone has identified that they are experiencing a problem of some kind and is speaking to someone, or about someone, who is involved in the problem.

Do they just discuss the problem and what happened to cause it, or do they apply some form of labelling to the person whose actions or behaviour they see as being the cause of the problem?

'John's such an idiot, he's messed up the payroll again.'

'Fatima, you're so messy, look at all the food and drink you've spilled on the table cloth. Why can't you be more careful?'

Take some time to notice whether you see others using labels about someone when they are discussing a problem that has happened.

If possible at the time, write down the sorts of things that have been said so that you can reconsider them later. How could they be restated by challenging the behaviour and not the person?

For example, the above statements could be rephrased as:

'The payroll has some errors in it again, I'll go and speak to John about it.'

'Fatima, can you clear up the food and drink you've spilled on the table please.'

These changes are very simple, but they do not label the person. The labelling in the original versions mean that those being spoken to or about are likely to resist both the label and any request (or order) that seeks to deal with the problem. You can perhaps see that Principle 1 - *that we treat each other with respect* also has relevance here.

The restated versions avoid the labelling and are far less likely to lead to resistance to the requests made to deal with the problem.

Listen out for these simple differences in how you, and others communicate. They can have a large impact on your ability to connect with others and to resolve difficult situations. The more you become mindful of these differences the more the Principle is likely to become part of your everyday language.

Make sure you consider your own labelling of others! This is the only contribution to communication you have control of in relation to this Principle. What labels have you applied to someone as a consequence of behaviours you have observed in them?

Whether negative labels or positive, to what extent has the label caused you to see the person in a fixed way, closed to variations in their behaviour?

What would you do, and how would you feel if the person you have positive labels for failed to live up to them one day? Would *they* be letting you down? It was your label after all, they didn't ask you to give it to them?

What if the person you have negative labels for (or a member of a group you associate with them) behaves in a way that contradicts those labels at some point? Do you have it within you to question the labels you have for them? Or will you find a way of dismissing your observation as a 'one-off' so that you can keep your label for them intact?

It was your label in the first place after all, so it can only be you that decides whether to keep it or change it. And as always, the consequences of your decision will also be yours.

Bear in mind that labels will not just be those that are recognised as being destructive stereotypes about race, religion, gender, sexuality etc. but also those we may overlook that we apply based on political persuasion, affluence, accent, job status or role ('corporate slave'), education 'level', family status or position, age-related ('typical teenager', 'OAP'), health status and any others.

Again, I want to emphasise this Principle isn't about being 'politically correct' in our statements for fear of offending someone, it is about whether we want our communication to be effective and whether we want a difficult situation to be resolved and a problem to be dealt with as immediately and simply as possible instead of descending into a time and energy sapping exchange of labels and potentially abusive comments.

And what about labels applied to you by others?
If you find someone else to be labelling *you* in a difficult situation and not your behaviour or something you have done, and as a consequence you are not fully clear about why they are giving you the label, an understanding of this Principle can help you to step back from being offended or upset by their label so that you can then ask a question such as:

What was it I did that led you to call me lazy/stupid/arrogant/a bully etc.?

What leads you to describe me as a 'typical teenager'?

You described me as a 'corporate slave', what have I done or what else leads you to call me that?

While personally challenging in that you may be upset by the label ascribed to you and you may, instead, simply wish to dismiss it or even seek to label the other person in return, if you can ask such a question it can enable a greater level of understanding from both of your perspectives about what has happened that the other person is concerned or upset by.

Once you have understood more about what you did that led them to apply the particular label to you, the easier it will be to move forward and resolve whatever led to the original difficulty.

Remember that hearing their reasons for applying the label to you doesn't mean you have to agree with them, it just means you have a better understanding of what has happened in the situation because you now have much more information than just a label to work with.

Your openness and willingness to explore what led to the label being applied, in contrast to being defensive and perhaps retaliating with a 'label for the labeller', is more likely to help resolution of any difficulty in the situation.

Defense is the first act of war - Byron Katie[20]

---

[20] www.thework.com

When you consider the alternative, of sticking with the 'tennis match' of labels and its ineffectiveness in moving forward over a difficult issue, it starts to become more and more clear why this Principle can be so useful in creating effective communication which, additionally, supports conflict resolution.

That we challenge the behaviour and not the person

Principle 7 Notes:

Principle 8: That we respect confidentiality

We create better quality communication if we respect confidentiality because of the trust and sense of safety that arises within our relationships when we do so. Someone is more likely to share thoughts and feelings and information that they might otherwise keep hidden when they feel the space in which they create their communication is a safe one.

If we are supporting someone in a difficult situation, we will be more able to do so if we maintain confidentiality, not because *we* now have access to more information, but because *they* have been able to express it, externalise it and start to reflect on what they can do about their difficulty. When a person doesn't feel safe to express their thoughts and feelings it is difficult for them to create a better way forward because they remain 'wrapped up inside'.

Putting the difficult thoughts and feelings 'out on the table' where they can be reviewed and worked on to create a better way forward from their difficulty can be a significant help in resolving personal conflict, whether the sharing occurs with the other person(s) involved in the difficult situation or is just shared with a respectful listener.

If I share something in confidence with someone, perhaps some personal information about my health, a difficulty I am experiencing, the details of a delicate situation I am involved in, how I feel about another person etc., and the person I share it with discusses that information with someone else without my consent, I am likely to be more cautious about being open in my communication with that person again in the future.

They have spoken on my behalf[21]. They have taken away from me my ownership[22] of what I choose to have shared with others. I feel disempowered[23] because of something happening that affects me, but which I had no control over.

If I do communicate with them again in the future, it is likely to be in a more superficial manner. I will be less likely to want to connect with them and may even avoid them to lessen the risk of further personal information being shared without my consent. I will do this to regain ownership of what I choose to share with others and to take back my power over my situation.

I have that power, to withhold information from someone. But the consequence of my decision to do so is a less meaningful connection between myself and the person I originally trusted with the information.

---

[21] www.communicationandconflict.com/speak-for.html
[22] www.communicationandconflict.com/ownership.html
[23] www.communicationandconflict.com/empowerment.html

I may feel upset that I have to do this but also that it is a necessary action to protect myself, and so the communication and relationship between us is far less intimate, trusting and open than it could be.

Often it will be as a result of 'idle gossip' that confidentiality has not been respected but the person sharing the information with others may not realise the impact of their actions, particularly if they do so on a frequent basis and it just feels 'normal' for them to do so.

Disregarding confidentiality is a cause of distress in many relationships, whether personal or professional:

- Ex-partners or friends may share information about us with others and as a consequence we may feel uneasy in the company of the ex-partner or friend *and* those they share the information with.

- Work colleagues may share information about us with others that we had hoped would be kept in confidence and this is often a cause of unease in the workplace.

- A social group we belong to such as a hobby group or a community group we are involved in may have members who have not considered the impact of sharing a personal issue such as a health or relationship difficulty we are experiencing with other members of the group.

Within the Helping Professions, clients may have information shared about them 'between professions' for safeguarding or other reasons but sometimes go on to find the information is subject to reinterpretation, leading to informal labelling[24] of the client as 'difficult' or in some other way 'of concern' or 'vulnerable'.

The client can start to feel inhibited about sharing important information about their situation because they feel that what they previously shared in trust has not been respected or has been used in ways they were not expecting.

While sharing information between professionals working with people is important for a range of different safety reasons and for other purposes, it can also be mistreated and not sufficiently considered with regard to how the information is used and how it affects the person or people concerned.

When this happens, it is to the detriment of all concerned as it means information is withheld by clients rather than shared with a sense of safety and respect for how it is treated, and this

---

[24] www.communicationandconflict.com/labels.html

withholding of information obstructs effective support being given.

In any context, our willingness to connect with those who do not respect confidentiality is inhibited because we do not feel safe to communicate with them. Sometimes it may not be our information that is shared inappropriately but because we witness the confidentiality of others' personal information being breached we feel inhibited with regard to sharing our own thoughts and experiences and circumstances.

If we are someone who has not respected confidentiality we can expect the likelihood of less open communication and connection from others, but sometimes may not understand why, unless we give this Principle sufficient consideration.

I live and work in London and travel on public transport and it is not uncommon for me to see a Solicitor working on an open file of correspondence on the tube with client addresses and other information easily readable over their shoulder. I have been on trains where social work professionals have used client names when discussing with other colleagues on their mobile phones the details of a situation they are dealing with. Even if I am not the client of these professionals, I am at risk of developing a lack of trust in the profession concerned with regard to their respect for the confidentiality of personal information.

I am also surprised in workplace settings where I hear professionals refer to individuals by name when they don't need to in order to make a point about something they are discussing. Instead of saying *'Fred Smith has an alcohol dependency'*, they can say, *'A client I am working with has an alcohol dependency'* unless the meeting is specifically about Fred Smith.

Of course, I am also at risk of *challenging the 'profession' and not the behaviour* by holding a generalised belief about solicitors and social workers unless I remind myself of Principle 7 and so I can take my own steps in any interaction with any professional I have concerns about to question their approach to confidentiality for my own self-assurance.

In some professional contexts there may be exceptions to the guarantee of confidentiality but where that is so, the exceptions can be explained to the client before any meeting so that they can decide what they wish to share. This has to be done verbally and if helpful, supplemented by a document so that it is clear that both participants understand what the exceptions are. Just giving a document and hoping the client reads it is not practising this Principle as it does not ensure a shared understanding of the exceptions because a discussion highlights whether the professional *also* understands them or not. If the exceptions are not clarified and information is shared by the professional anyway because they do not understand the exceptions it remains a breach of confidentiality and unprofessional conduct.

When the listener and the speaker know and mutually understand any exceptions to a guarantee of confidentiality a trust is developed in any relationship whether personal or professional through appropriately practising this Principle.

Confidentiality and Conflict Resolution

A commitment to respecting confidentiality explains why this Principle is also very significant in supporting people in resolving their conflicts. People have often lost trust in others when they are in a dispute, and feel unable to say how they feel and what they think, through fear it will be shared and misinterpreted, and possibly used to condemn them.

A demonstrated commitment to maintaining confidentiality by a mediator or conflict coach or anyone trying to help another to resolve a conflict provides a sanctuary for them. They can discuss the issues, feelings, events or experiences that have had to be 'kept hidden' from others.

Being listened to[25], in confidence, provides the opportunity for someone to lay out their concerns 'on the table' so that they can review them and 'get their head around' their situation, without fear that their thoughts and feelings will be told to others.

---

25 www.communicationandconflict.com/listening.html

This can be the first step towards creating a new way forward in a difficult situation. It provides an opportunity for honest, open reconsideration of their situation, without a need to be guarded about what they say, or a need to justify their actions, because whatever they say will be heard in confidence and not shared with others or used to condemn them in some way.

The practice of respecting confidentiality can be carried out by all of us, both in our own communications with others and in our attempts to help others with some difficulty they are experiencing.

But how often do we acknowledge the importance of confidentiality and make a commitment to providing a confidential, safe space for someone to share their thoughts, feelings and concerns, without fear that we will then share them with others?

This is another example of where 'making it a rule' to respect confidentiality is insufficient as it is likely to lead to a 'confidentiality policy' in some contexts that, in turn, leads to an assumption that the practice exists with no further thought or reflection given to whether it does or not.

Each of us is *individually* responsible for respecting confidentiality through developing a mindfulness about our own communication practices. Our commitment to practising this

Principle has to arise from our own wish to create more effective communication, if we have that wish, and not because a policy tells us to.

Principle 8 Challenge:

The following questions are intended to help you consider various aspects of the relevance and application of the Principle *that we respect confidentiality* so that you can develop an awareness, a *mindfulness* regarding its contribution to your creation of effective communication.

Consider the relevance and impact of confidentiality in both your personal life and your professional life:

- What are the challenges and temptations that prevent you from respecting confidentiality?

- How much focused consideration have you given to confidentiality in the past, whether in your personal life or your professional life?

- What can you learn from your answers to that question?

- In what situations do you find yourself concerned about confidentiality?

- What are the feelings, thoughts, experiences, even 'pastimes' that you would not want to have divulged to anyone other than someone you can trust to keep them confidential?

- To what extent do you consider others' similar needs for confidentiality when they share something with you?

- How do you establish whether something needs to be kept confidential or not, whether something you wish to share with others or something they share with you?

Please remember that there are not 'right' and 'wrong' answers to these questions. Your answers will help you consider whether there are consequences to your communication practices that you have not recognised before, and whether there are changes that you would want to make after taking the opportunity to reflect on what you do presently.

Principle 8 Notes:

Principle 9: That it is ok to make mistakes because they are opportunities for learning

This Principle acknowledges that communication is a creative process and as such is open to continued review and change, sometimes improvement, and sometimes deterioration. It also recognises that the communication we create will be unique to each relationship it helps to form. It is through our mindfulness in relation to our communication that we can seek to learn from mistakes and maintain our creativity, and in turn be more likely to grow through our experience of conflict.

It would be a contradiction for the Principles in this book to be 'rules' as if they *must* be followed. They are Principles because they give an insight into what contributes to the creation of effective communication and why. But it's important to note that it may not always be possible to practise them and that it's ok to make mistakes in our communication, whether that means in not practising the Principles, or in other ways.

What does matter is that we are aware, or *mindful* of *how* we have communicated, and through understanding the Principles we can become more aware of the consequences of using them or not using them. In this way we can take responsibility for our contribution to communication and its consequences.

This supports our empowerment in any given interaction as well as the likelihood of a creative resolution of any conflict that arises within it.

If we were to consider the Principles to be 'rules' it risks their practice being seen as *something you must do* and blindly follow without any need for understanding of the reasons why. In this way the mindfulness of the communication would be lost.

If we treat the Principles as 'rules' we may also start to criticise others for 'not following the rules', volunteering them to use them, rather than see how awareness of the Principles helps *us* to be more consciously aware of our own part in creating communication with others whether they practise the Principles or not.

The Principles are not for imposition on others, they *have the right to pass* on practising them. Indeed, they may have no interest in them at all and so if we *volunteer others* to practise them we are, ourselves, not practising the Principles. The Principles are a tool, not a 'moral code'.

I often hear people in dispute say *'Well the problem is they are a bad communicator'* and so they locate the cause of their difficulty or relationship breakdown in the other person. But of course, in doing so they are challenging the person not the behaviour and speaking for others - *and* abdicating responsibility for their part in not managing to create effective communication with the other person.

And this is a further issue that arises when we believe there are 'rules' to how we communicate or even that there is a 'science' to it. We see ourselves as following the rules and others as not following them - and then we shut down communication by suggesting the other person is not 'playing the game', rather than continue to strive for a deeper understanding of the other person, of ourselves and of the situation we are communicating about, *because it is in our own interests* to create a better way forward.

There is only communication, and communication is a shared creation by two or more people. The idea that there is a 'good communicator' and a 'bad communicator' is a blame-focused perspective that obstructs the creative process that constitutes communication.

> *"As to methods there may be a million and then some, but principles are few. The man who grasps principles can successfully select his own methods. The man who tries methods, ignoring principles, is sure to have trouble."* - **Ralph Waldo Emerson** - who perhaps, if he made his important observation today, would be less gender-specific in expressing it.

The purpose of the challenges given after each of the Principles is to help you see the consequences of practising, or not practising each of them so that you become more mindful of how *you* are contributing to, or inhibiting the creation of effective communication in your daily interactions with others, particularly if any of those interactions relate to a presently unresolved conflict or have the potential to lead to one.

It's ok to make mistakes! That's why the challenges are called challenges and not 'Tests' where you get a score depending on how many you got 'wrong' or 'right'. Some days you will practise the Principles and on other days you won't because of personal or circumstantial issues that affect your ability to do so. What matters is your awareness of when you are and when you are not. In practising the Principles and in all other areas of our lives it's important that we can make mistakes and be open and honest about them. When this is so the mistakes become great opportunities for learning:

> *"Recently I was asked if I was going to fire an employee who made a mistake that cost the company $600,000. No, I replied, I just spent $600,000 training him."* **Thomas J.Watson, founder of IBM**

When it's not ok to make mistakes, a lot of time and energy is spent allocating blame for the mistake that has happened, instead of immediately seeking the learning that can be gained from it.

Instead of *'Oh no, who did that?'* our concern becomes *'Oh no how did that happen?'* if we are to use the situation as an opportunity for learning.

And then we can see if the answer is *'John did it!'* even though we asked *'How did that happen?'*. If we do get a response about who was involved with little, if any, information about what happened then we are not going to be able to learn from the situation. When the focus continues to be on 'who' did something with little interest in the circumstances and events that led to a problem occurring then we know that we find ourselves in a 'blame environment'.

If we are in a no-blame environment[26], the person who made the mistake will feel safe enough to say *'I left the door open and the dog got through into the kitchen'.*

To this the response can be:

'Ok, well let's clear up the mess and then look at how we can stop this happening again in the future.'

---

[26] www.communicationandconflict.com/no-blame.html

not .... *'John you are so dozy and clumsy, you are grounded, go to your room and don't come out until it's time for dinner'.*

Grounding John means he doesn't get a chance to contribute to making amends for his mistake. It means we have to clear the mess up ourselves and it doesn't include any provision for learning how to prevent it happening again in the future. This is because our focus has not been on finding out how it happened and learning from it, it has been on allocating blame and punishment and challenging the person not the behaviour.

Take a moment to pause and think about how often the latter response happens in your own life and in situations you find yourself in, whether that is your own response or that of others you are with.

So much opportunity for learning, change and growth is lost when it's not ok to make mistakes.

Further to this, in a blame environment, where mistakes aren't ok, the chances are high that John will look to pass the blame to others, perhaps to say that it was not his fault, it was Jamie's. Jamie was pushing him and he had to run away before he could close the door.

And we could get involved in an investigation to find out whose fault it *really* is so that we know who must go to their room, and possibly in the end send both John and Jamie to their rooms because it seems 'easier'.

Meanwhile the mess is still there and now there are even fewer people around to help clear up, and those that were around have started fighting in their room. We can hear the thumping and shouting.

And still we haven't learned how to prevent it happening again in the future!

You may be able to think of similar scenarios playing out in other walks of life - at work, in the community, in politics, internationally!

Take a moment to consider those situations. How much learning happened? How much unresolved conflict and recriminations and finger-pointing at individuals or groups remains? How likely is it that the same situation will happen again?

Unfortunately, many of those situations are much more serious than a dog getting through into the kitchen and causing a mess, and far more wasted effort goes into finding someone to blame while desperately little goes into clearing up the mess and finding out what can be learned to prevent it happening again in the future.

A communication approach that does not allow for mistakes means that people will be unlikely to acknowledge and communicate about their failings and vulnerabilities. As a consequence, little will change as there is no opportunity for review and creation of better ways of doing things.

Communication will be minimal in such an environment because there will be a lack of trust that anything said will not be used to condemn the speaker. Blame will be the main response to any problem that arises and stagnation will result as no new insights will be gained if there is little, or any review of the causes of the problem, just a search for *'Who did it, who is to blame?'*. What usually then follows is a punishment, a sacking, a sanction or condemnation with the suggestion that that has now 'dealt with' the problem, when of course it hasn't – because nothing has been learned that will help to prevent it happening again in the future.

In a no-blame environment where it is ok to make mistakes, the situation can become a 'shared puzzle', a curiosity, a learning opportunity, a challenge to be overcome in order to lead to improvement, including in situations where the consequences are very serious. Indeed, their severity means it is even more important that a no-blame approach is taken – where mistakes can be openly acknowledged with a view to gaining the greatest understanding of what led to a problem situation arising so that improvements and change can occur.

Where a focus on mistakes is in order to allocate the greatest and least level of 'blame' it is unlikely the influential factors and circumstances that led to the situation arising will even be acknowledged and shared.

We can condemn people for 'not owning up', but if the environment we create in which we expect them to is **not** one where *it is ok to make mistakes because they can be opportunities for learning,* why would we be surprised by their reluctance to 'own up'?

Thomas J. Watson again, founder of IBM:

> *Would you like me to give you a formula for success? It's quite simple, really. Double your rate of failure.*

My thanks to Tim Ferris[27], author of *The 4 hour Work Week* for the quotes by Thomas J.Watson.

But while the quotes are taken from business contexts, the underlying thinking applies to all situations. Our relationships would be much more peaceful and fulfilling if we were able to accept mistakes in ourselves, and others, and treat them as opportunities for learning.

---

[27] fourhourworkweek.com

You may be thinking: '*Well it would be nice to be in such an environment but it doesn't happen here.*'

As with all of the Principles, their practice starts with us, and we choose to practise them for ourselves, and with others, or not. And once we understand the consequences of practising them, or not, we can take responsibility for our part in those consequences. Or not!

Whether we do or not, the consequences will remain and if we don't accept responsibility for our part we will retain a sense of powerlessness about our interactions with others.

Can I adopt a no-blame approach which accepts that it is ok to make mistakes, that treats them as opportunities for learning?

Can I apply this to myself?

If not me then who?

That's the Challenge for Principle 9 and to take beyond the completion of this book!

> *You must be the change you want to see in the world.*
> **Mahatma Gandhi**

About the Author

Alan Sharland has been a Mediator since 1994, starting as a volunteer Mediator for Camden Mediation Service in London, UK. Prior to this he was a Teacher of Mathematics in a Secondary School in Camden. His involvement in mediation arose from trying to understand more about conflict as a result of a pupil from the school he worked in being murdered by a group of youths. Many of his pupils had been involved in violence either as victims or perpetrators and sometimes both.

Working with people involved in destructive conflicts in his role as a Mediator enabled Alan to recognise common behaviours and approaches that typify ineffective responses to conflict. Mediation seeks to enable more effective responses to be created by those involved in a dispute, complaint or other difficulty. Observing how participants in the mediation process moved on to create more effective ways forward for themselves gave the material for the content in this book and evolved into the Principles that inform how Alan practises as a Mediator and Conflict Coach and how he trains others to be Mediators and Conflict Coaches.

Alan had an upbringing where arguments were frequent but love was never absent. Disagreements never led to continued resentment or aggression or violence, and for this continuous foundation of love he thanks his late parents Derek Sharland and Marjorie Sharland and his two older brothers Andy and Paul. Seeing others' arguments and feeling he had the answer to resolve them proved difficult when his 'solutions' weren't taken on board.

This taught Alan that 'taking on' others' difficulties only increases the complexity and number of problems present in a dispute as it means one more person is simply adding their frustrations to the mix. Understanding that conflict is inevitable and trusting that people always have the capacity to resolve their own disputes was one of the greatest challenges he faced and still faces as a Mediator and Conflict Coach.

Alan says:
"*A Guide to Effective Communication for Conflict Resolution* enables the reader, first of all, to just notice their present approach to communication. It introduces the Principles, explains them through examples and then encourages the reader to practise the Principles in their own communication.

In essence the Principles are simple, but they are personally challenging because they cause us to reassess what may be common practices in our everyday communication. It is important to notice these common practices in ourselves and others first of all, to see how prevalent and unconscious they are. Once we have become more conscious or 'mindful' about our communication we can apply the Principles to our day-to-day interactions and see the difference in others' responses to us, as well as in our own contributions to communication. We then see how practising the Principles can lead to a greater sense of connection and more creative responses to the inevitable conflicts we experience with others."

Other Publications by Alan Sharland

How to Resolve Bullying in the Workplace - *Stepping Out of The Circle of Blame to Create an Effective Outcome for All*

Websites:
www.communicationandconflict.com
www.caos-conflict-management.co.uk
caotica.caos-conflict-management.co.uk

Communication and Conflict youtube channel:
http://bit.ly/ComnCon

Connect with Alan Sharland

Thank you for reading my book!

Here are my social media pages in case you would like to make contact:

CAOS Conflict Management on Facebook:
www.facebook.com/CAOS.Conflict.Management

Communication and Conflict on Facebook:
www.facebook.com/communicationandconflict

Follow Alan on Twitter:
twitter.com/alan_sharland

Connect on LinkedIn:
www.linkedin.com/in/alansharland

Please email Alan with any questions or comments you have about this book or his work at CAOS Conflict Management:

caos@caos-conflict-management.co.uk

CAOS CONFLICT MANAGEMENT

PROMOTING MINDFUL COMMUNICATION
GROWTH THROUGH CONFLICT

TEL. 020 3371 7507
LONDON, UNITED KINGDOM

WWW.CAOS-CONFLICT-MANAGEMENT.CO.UK

Printed in Great Britain
by Amazon

29655656R00095